STAMINA

STAMINA

Derek Anderson

Cover Design by: Trevis Smith
Copy editing by: Alyssa M. Curry

ISBN 13: 978-0-615824-30-7

For information regarding special discounts for bulk purchases of this book for educational or gift purposes, as a charitable donation, or to arrange a speaking event with the author, please contact:

www.derekandersonworks.com
twitter @DerekLAnderson
www.facebook.com/derekandersonworks

DEDICATION

I dedicate this book to all my schoolteachers, basketball coaches, helping friends, male and female mentors, my children, my parents, my closest friend Terrance Stewart, the Masser Family, my Uncle George, and most of all.... God. Thank you all for believing in me!

LOVE & LOYALTY
Derek

I knew Derek was smarter then he acted and once he got his first A in my class, I knew he was destined to be someone the world would know and love.

~ Mrs.McGill
Derek's Middle School Social Studies Teacher

Derek has overcome a lot in his life but he never made excuses when it came down to getting things done. He always wanted to be the best at everything and he never complained one time while always smiling. You would never know his situation because he didn't allow his situation to stop him.

~Kevin Salyer
Doss High School Basketball Coach

If it's one person that god had a plan for it was Derek. He had to grow up with no parents while being a parent at age 14. There is only a select few that get chosen to survive that much and still be successful as Derek.

~ Terrance Moorman
Derek's Childhood Mentor

I always knew Derek had a gift but I never let him forget what hard work meant. I wanted him to be a better person then a basketball player so that's what I focused on more than anything. I think he exceeded both of our expectations. Very proud of my nephew!

~ George Williams
Derek's Uncle

Introduction

It's June 20, 2006 in Dallas, Texas and Game 6 of the NBA finals. There are twenty-two thousand fans on their feet screaming and shouting at my Miami Heat teammates and I. We're in the American Airlines Arena, home to the NBA Dallas Mavericks. Eight huge video screens flash court views from on top the oddly curved ceiling. The noise is deafening. It's virtually too hot to breathe on the floor and the eruption of voices continues to grow louder.

It has been an amazing comeback. We were down two games to none and most people counted us out. No team had ever comeback from that kind of deficit before. Media all across the country said we were through. However, the turning point came in Game 3 when we overcame a thirteen-point deficit with less than six minutes remaining in the fourth quarter to win 98–96. The experience of making our dream come alive was far more inconceivable than I could have imagined.

At that point, victory was practically ours. We were ahead by two points with .09 seconds on the game clock. I stood on the sideline, when it hit me that there wasn't another team in history that had done what we were about to do. Thousands of people were standing, screaming, pointing, or waving their hands victoriously in the air. My teammates and I could barely restrain our energy or hold back from rushing the court in celebration. That very moment was nothing less than amazing. As I watched my teammate get fouled and begin to shoot the free throws, I glanced into the wildly cheering crowd for a brief second and couldn't help but stop and reflect on my journey from my earliest childhood to *this* moment.

I had won championships from middle school, high school, college, and the Junior Olympics. I was at the pinnacle of my career and about to achieve victory on the greatest stage of my life, the NBA finals. For a split second, as I looked around the arena and focused on the faces so full of intense emotion, I was drawn back to seeing the agony in my mother's face as she cried out in misery in a drug rehab center. I recalled my father barely able to smile through the incessant pain of lung cancer as he struggled for his life. The shocking memory of my sister dying in agony, reaching up to grab her daughter's hand, as my father's best friend stabbed her seventeen times. I envisioned my brother trying to force a smile although I had not seen him since we were children many years ago.

My memory pulled me back to when I was an eleven-year-old boy that had to live alone without food or electricity for numerous days. As my memory progressed there was a twelve-year-old child who had to sleep on a hard park bench for way too many nights. There was a fourteen-year-old boy who had a child while he was still a child. I recalled him raising that child as a single parent. I remembered a teenaged boy stabbed in his back as he ran for his life. I see all of those people standing in the crowd and then realize; they are all me.

I gripped my towel and looked down at the floor trying to acknowledge that person doesn't exist anymore. He's gone, although the recollections of my journey remain. Those memories and the faces in them are of my past. Tonight, we have the opportunity to win and I finally comprehend that my life has a purpose even when I didn't know what it was.

I'm quickly pulled back to the game. The Mav's grab an opportunity to tie it. There's only enough time on the clock for one last shot. Will we get our first NBA Title? The Maverick player takes the shot and misses as the clock ticks to zero. We won! The ball is thrown straight up into the air as the buzzer sounds, and we storm the floor as NBA Champions! We flooded onto the court pounding each other on the back and embracing one another as our tears flow heavily and freely. Reporters, friends, and family members rushed the court. It was a madhouse.

Finally, the melee on the court subsided and I walked into the locker room with my teammates to celebrate. We poured champagne all over the room and on each other. Within minutes, my teammate's family members, our staff, and hordes of news reporters entered the locker room. I had no one. I hadn't thought our victory would come in Game 6, so my friends and family remained at home. I was already used to the deep feeling of impending loneliness. From my earliest games, neither my mother nor father ever came to see me play. Drugs and alcohol had taken so much from our family that my parents had become unknown to my basketball career for several years. I never saw their faces in the stands or experienced the happiness that my teammates were able to share with their loved ones. It would have been of great comfort to feel it. There were periods in my life that I've had tremendous success and still couldn't stop or defeat my feeling of loneliness, but I had faith that it would strengthen me. I put aside the loneliness that had been my constant companion for the duration of my life and celebrated the victory that my faith and determination has brought me thus far.

I walked to the bathroom to wipe the champagne out of my burning eyes and stood in the mirror staring at my reflection. Since childhood, I've been the only one able to see my face without the mask I've worn to hide my pain. When I went to school I didn't want people to know my struggles, so I'd smile. In the neighborhood, I'd sit quietly trying to remain inconspicuous so no one became aware of the many problems I had. It didn't take much for me to entertain the thought of how far I'd come. My reflection displayed the sacrifices, disappointments, loneliness, pain and sadness, yet through it all, I was still able to see that I survived everything. I wasn't left in the shelter home after my parents abandoned me. I didn't burn to death in either of our house fires. At merely sixteen, walking my two-year-old son to work with me in freezing cold weather, we managed. None of those things mattered any longer because I learned the greatest lesson we can learn in life; never stop believing in yourself and never run out of breath to fight for your life! *I had proven that I had the stamina to endure it all.*

At one point, I was a product of my environment but in time I made my environment a product of me. I've learned to eliminate the excuses that today our youth use to justify their failure. If you want to get out of your situation you can, but *you* must decide to do so. I didn't blame the problems I encountered throughout my life on my parents' inability to raise me. I didn't use the fact that I lived in my neighborhood as the reason I lived in poverty, and I don't fault myself for making child-like decisions when I was a child. I never blamed anything or anyone for my decisions because they were my decisions alone. The way I see it is regardless of your gender you can't make excuses for your life because life isn't the one to blame. That's my way of saying *you* are responsible for your life and the decisions that affect it. Nevertheless, that life must be lived with a purpose and if you live it correctly, you can accomplish your dreams and conquer your nightmares.

The purpose for this book isn't to make people feel bad for me because of my childhood. What I hope to reveal is a blueprint on how to make the most out of what you have. Additionally, I want to instill in you the power of not giving credence or thought to the concept of quitting before you win the ultimate prize. That prize is the success you can create for yourself and it will last a lifetime, regardless of your past.

Throughout life, my opponents consisted of poverty, loneliness, disappointment, jealously, and lack of equal educational opportunities. As I learned from playing basketball, life is about how bad you want to win, how much time you're willing to put into making your dreams become a reality, and how much you are willing to sacrifice now for your success later. I've won on every level of basketball but my biggest accomplishments are being a good father, a good person, and a great child of God. I'm just getting warmed up to win my last championship, and to bring home the best trophy ever... My Legacy!

I wrote Stamina so that it would be a source of inspiration and strength to everyone who reads it.

What follows is my story.

Chapter 1

THE LONG RUN BEGINS

I didn't grow up like a lot of other children. Scratch that! I did grow up like many children but the difference was that I wanted to be more than most kids. My journey can be seen as tough, hurtful, embarrassing, and unfair because it felt that way at the time I was experiencing it. Looking back, it turned out that God had a plan for my life. It was *constructed* to help make me resilient, hurtful but rendered me *pain free*, embarrassing except I was *not ashamed*, and unfair although I was *treated fairly*. I had every reason to feel bad about all the negative things that happened to me. I could've resented the way we lived and the manner I was forced to grow up, but I wanted to create a new path and then write my story. That meant I had to make the choice to do things that would change my situation and not let my situation change me!

From my perspective, I witnessed the worst living imaginable at a fledgling age. It should have made me bitter and angry but it didn't. What I experienced made me a better person. My thinking is this; if we never struggle, we will never learn how to get out of negative situations. If we don't encounter problems, we won't determine how to solve them later in life. On a spiritual level, if God never showed us we needed Him, would we ever call on Him?

I grew up in Flint, Michigan in the early 1970's and it seemed pretty normal to me. When you're barely eight-years-old you aren't aware that your city is the poster child for poverty, violence, and urban decay. Flint was once the proud home of General Motors, but decades of "white flight" and the collapse of the auto industry turned it into one of the worst places in the country to grow up.

I was a little kid in Flint, going through life's typical ups and downs. At least that's what I thought until I came home and found two dead men slumped over in their car. It was parked right in front of our apartment in the project housing on Carpenter Road. Where we lived, the brick buildings were attached and had metal doors. Everything was constructed of a dark brown brick. When you walked into our apartment, the kitchen met you straight ahead and the living area was to your immediate right. To the left was a flight of stairs that led up to three bedrooms.

Many of the units were boarded up. At a glance, the area that I lived in appeared abandoned. With all the bars on the windows and doors it looked like we were in prison. Our prison came complete with police from a nearby station, but they rarely interacted with the people in my neighborhood. It didn't appear that they ever came to help. Everyone knew they could do anything they wanted, so crime and drugs just got worse and worse.

My neighborhood was a dangerous place to live, but most of the time we were too young to know what was going on in the neighborhood, or even in our own houses. After school, we went outside and played football. We didn't actually have a football so we'd take a T-shirt, ball it up, and throw it. None of us had sneakers that fit and we didn't have the luxury of possessing actual sporting goods, but back then kids could make a game out of anything. We'd put a milk crate up on a telephone pole and used the balled up shirt to shoot at it, like basketball. We'd pitch rocks to see who came closest to the curb and played hide and seek to pass the time. One of the mischievous things we did was take off running around the buildings and knock on doors, only to run away as fast as possible before someone answered. This is what I called fun.

My mother was a beautiful woman in her early thirties, tall and statuesque. She had a light caramel complexion, with fine features, long black hair, and dimples that anyone would envy. She had a lovely figure and a radiant smile that could touch anyone's soul.

My father was a handsome man. He was huge and stood over 6'9. He was imposing and strong like a warrior chieftain. He had gone to fight in the Vietnam War in the 1960's and didn't come back until the early 1970's. The effect of that war left its scars on him the way it had so many others. I only have one picture of him in the military wearing his Army uniform, standing on top of a tank, with a big smile. Even at that height he operated a tank. There was no sign of him being hot-tempered or any display of the violence that was to come. He just looked like a guy who was serving his country and couldn't wait to return home to his family.

It wasn't difficult to see that my brother and I had different fathers. My brother looked just like his father. He was short, very light-skinned, and slightly built. It appeared odd that we actually had the same mother. People never thought we were related because I was so brown and tall and he was so short and light. Apart from our physical differences we were very dissimilar in our personalities. I was levelheaded and quiet. I always wanted to learn more about history as my father was into western cowboys and pop music. I spent countless hours listening to his albums and reading his cowboy books that he ordered for many years. To the contrary, my brother was quick-tempered and filled with anger most of the time. He would tear things apart just so he could put them back together.

From my earliest recollections, conflict ran rampant in our house. My father had become involved in street activity and did things that were constituted as violent. When my mother confronted him about his behaviors he became enraged. The yelling began and it didn't take long before he was hitting her. My brother and I listened to the unsettling sounds of their arguing and things breaking for hours on end before it subsided. We didn't have a choice but to stand by helplessly, hurt, and angry, while being unable to prevent it. Hearing the sounds of my mother being abused by my father caused a pain that ran so deep inside my spirit I would do anything to stop it. My brother would turn the volume up on the television to try and deafen the sound while I'd stare out the window into space trying to block it all out.

One time, the fighting went on for so many hours that we thought they were going to kill each other. Suddenly, there was an eerie dead silence interrupted by the sound of the front door slamming. We waited in complete silence afraid of what was taking place. Then, there was a loud boom! Our mother kicked in our bedroom door and told us to grab everything we could and be ready to leave at once. Her face was covered with bruises. We knew she was serious about leaving my father that time.

My brother and I frantically packed as much as we could, stuffing our belongings into suitcases. It seemed as though we waited in our room with our bags packed for hours anxiously awaiting our mother's next move. By the time she nervously crept back into our room it was extremely late. She told us to be quiet and follow closely behind her as we snuck out of the house. There was a cab waiting outside. We got in and my mother screamed at the driver to speed off. This was typical for us because we'd done it before when our parents fought. Usually, we stayed overnight with our mother's friend but somehow I knew this time was different.

We pulled up to the Greyhound bus station and my mother bought us tickets to Louisville, Kentucky where her mother and grandmother lived. We were used to them breaking up but I had never seen my mother so uneasy and scared. She fussed at us about everything. She said, "Don't sit by the window," or "Don't be looking around," and "Sit still and be quiet!" Even when we were getting on the bus, she pushed my brother and I down while she looked around in discernible fear. My mother wasn't the scared type but that night I saw how afraid she was. It was evident she was worried about the violence that could follow her.

We arrived at the Greyhound station just a few blocks away from our great-grandmother's apartment. The neighborhood was the first housing project ever built in the downtown area of Louisville. It was built so workers could walk to their cleaning and cooking jobs in the downtown office buildings. I thought the buildings were pretty old and they were made of cinderblock siding.

It didn't take long for us to settle in with my grandmother who was living with my great-grandmother at the time. My grandmother was the best at nurturing our family. My great-grandmother was a very stern and strong-minded lady who had to raise three generations of our family with only an eighth-grade education.

I remember the times we'd visit my great-grandmother. She'd constantly remind us to be thankful for what we had instead of complaining about what we didn't have. She'd always tell us, "Straighten your shoulders up in confidence," and there were times she'd say, "Stick your chin up and be proud of who you are." She had a very strong will that was passed down to all of her children. My great-grandmother was born in 1902 and was very strict in her ways. She was the rock of our family, as she had to move her three siblings from Casey County, outside of Danville, Kentucky to Louisville, Kentucky. They were forced to move after they witnessed their brother being dragged from the back of a pick-up truck because he looked at a white woman. Her parents were on the run from trying to hide her brother and they fled from Tennessee to Kentucky. She told us this story and made sure we never forgot how far we came to make it. My mother and grandmother didn't pay too much attention to that because they began to live in the ways of the world.

My mother would get into arguments with my great-grandmother and then pack up and leave without telling us if or when she was coming back.

One day, my mother had an extremely violent argument with my great-grandmother. My brother and I heard a sudden outbreak of loud smashing and then the crashing of glass being broken. We slipped down the steps and saw broken windows and a dusty old ax lying on the ground. Our great-grandmother was still shouting at my mother. My mother slammed the door and they continued their shouting match through the broken window. My brother and I quietly crept back upstairs and didn't say one word to each other. It was clear he was becoming frustrated with our mother. Unfortunately, I was still too young to understand how badly our family was falling apart. That was the final week we stayed at my great-grandmother's home.

A week later my mother came in and told us to pack our things because we were leaving. My mother struggled to get her clothes out of the closet. My brother and I watched her stagger around while trying to remain quiet. When she was packed, we snuck out of the house the exact same way we left Flint. It was becoming a regular routine for us to move around as if we were fugitives in our own family.

Sadly, after leaving my great-grandmother's home we moved four different times the following year. My mother relocated us from one place to another without any structure or stability. She intentionally isolated herself from her family because of her lifestyle and the men she chose. There were a lot of "aunts" or "uncles" we rarely ever saw. My brother and I became so immune to sudden changes that we didn't consider unpacking our things or have a chance to make new friends. Out of nowhere my father would reappear and we'd move in with him. It surprised me but it enraged my brother so he didn't speak to my father. He'd avoid his icy gaze as if they were enemies. My father would yell at him but he'd remain steadfast in his returned defiance.

The constant tension led to significant explosions. There was an occasion that my brother came in late one night and my father hit him. My mother reacted angrily by punching my father dead in his face, which was guaranteed to cause a fight. While my brother ran to our room and began packing his things I returned to the living room only to find my father sitting on top of my mother with his hands firmly wrapped around her neck, choking her. Without a thought, I jumped on his back in an attempt to stop him but I was too small to fight him or pull him off of my mother. I was infuriated! With every ounce of strength I could assemble, I tried to grip my hands around *his* throat. In one swift brutal reaction, he pushed me so hard that I slammed into the coffee table and banged my head against it. When I reached up to assess the damage to my throbbing head, bright red blood covered my hand. The noise brought my brother tearing into the living room in an effort to help. Before we had a chance to react my father stood up, angrily towered over us, and demanded we return to our room.

After my mother managed to get up from their fight she rushed into the room and instructed us to finish packing our things and then left. We waited for her to get us but it didn't take long for them to commence with their vicious argument. Suddenly, we heard a man's voice arguing with my father. It was my mother's brother, George, who had always been the dominant man in our family. Several minutes later our mother came to get us. We went downstairs and my father and uncle were standing practically face-to-face. My uncle was staring a hole straight through my father as he fearlessly ushered us past him. In a low and dark tone George said to my father, "If you ever put your hands on my family again, I will kill you myself." I knew he meant it.

I'd never heard anyone speak to my father in that manner and to hear my uncle actually threaten him gave my brother and me a sense of protection we never had before. What we found surprising was that my mother never got along with my uncle, but for some reason when it came to her children, he'd die trying to protect us. Unfortunately, she abused her relationship with my uncle George far too many times and after a while their relationship deteriorated like all of the others.

LIFE: If you've ever been abused and ultimately surrendered to that type of unhealthy and life-threatening relationship, ask yourself this question. If you saw a man beating a woman, would you help her or call for help? In that situation, most people would call the police or do something to help, yet refuse to help themselves. I find this difficult to comprehend because it's implausible to think of anyone staying with a person who abuses your love. You're the one making the choice to stay because you don't want to hear what others will think about you or how it will affect your finances. Many, simply don't want to start over and take a chance on building another relationship. You may use these as excuses to justify your choice of living in fear of change, but there is no comparison to fearing for your life.

Make a "To-do" list, put yourself on it and then take the steps to actually take care of *yourself*. It shouldn't matter if you like it or not, people are going to talk about you. They may be proud of you for making the change or gossip while being ill-informed of your situation. If Hilary Clinton can deal with her husband cheating on her on a platform so large that the entire world knows about it, I'm sure your handful of gossipers won't disrupt your spirit for long. If you have children, consider that they will be better off being removed from a violent or unhealthy environment in which the very behaviors that are practiced are learned. Teach them to be respectful from the time they are able to talk. Instill in them the power of forgiveness and not to hold onto hatred for what has occurred. Explain to them that it's in the past. Doing so will allow your children to be open to having a positive role model to help guide them at a point they may need it the most. Don't prepare your child to grow up angry and have little to no trust or faith. Allowing them to hear, witness, or fight your battles could cause them more harm that may take years to correct, if at all. Don't allow your children to learn how to sing a song before they can recite and understand a prayer. The majority of children prefer to feel their parents love with unwavering certainty more than they would a gift. Take time to discern what it is that your children should have or need, and then provide it.

My mother missed out on a great deal of enjoyment in my life because of the pain she endured and held onto. Don't lose yourself in an abusive relationship because there is always someone willing to help. While I would have given anything to be the man my mother loved more than anyone in the world she couldn't see beyond her own pain and missed out on the joys I fought to have. The choices we make are sometimes extremely emotional, which is the worst time to make one. How we handle the results from our choices typically reveal what our character is like.

It's okay to learn from making mistakes because we all have our vices but never allow yourself to lose the love of your true friends and family. Of course, it seems as though it's easier said than done. However, consider that there are countless men that would love to wrap their arms around you to caress and hold you as oppose to choking you in a fit of uncontrolled rage. Take time to understand yourself and who you want to become so that you may evolve to having a discerning spirit about people before allowing them to hurt you or your family.

Women have more power and value than they know and now it's time to focus on building up our women instead of beating them down in anger. Women need to realize that the ordinary, respectful man you may pass over will be the exact same man you will want to be with after dealing with the immature, selfish and abusive man you continue to chase. A man should take care in finding a woman instead of hunting one to serve his purposes.

* * *

Chapter 2

FIGHTING FOR ENDURANCE

Our last move as a family happened to take us to a place where I believed only the strongest of people could live. The housing project called, "Peyton Place" also known as, "Little Africa" put us in a horrific environment and carried the same old abandoned look as my great-grandmother's building. There was added tension deriving from the surrounding project houses next to ours. The community consisted of a borough of three housing projects with a Police Precinct situated in the middle of them. The other two were called Southwick and Cotter Homes. There was a grocery store, gas station, and a few mom and pop stores. An old house masquerading as a restaurant separated the housing projects and low-income houses. Like most poor urban neighborhoods, we had at least three liquor stores and a Laundromat that looked like a social club at times because so many people went there during the weekends.

I was nearly eleven and Peyton Place was supposed to be a new start for us. My mother began to receive government aid and stay home the majority of time. Life was already beginning to change.

I recall our first Christmas Eve there. My brother and I raced home from playing outside. We couldn't hold in our excitement because Christmas was the following day. Once we entered the apartment we were completely disheartened to find that there wasn't a single gift anywhere in the small living room. Although a little disappointed, we calmly went into our room as my mother sat emotionless on the sofa watching television the duration of the night. When we began talking about the situation my brother became upset that there weren't any gifts. I tried to calm him down and defuse his rising irritation by telling him they were probably hidden somewhere in the apartment, but after taking a look at reality he blared out, "Where would they be then?" He had a point. I left the room and walked into the kitchen to get a glass of water trying not to bother my mother. On my way back to the room my curiosity claimed the best of me and I tried to ask her a question. Before I could get it out she interrupted me and said, "I don't want to hear it. Go to bed."

My brother and I woke up on Christmas morning to find the same thing as the night before, nothing. I could tell that times were particularly hard for my mother, but later that day her new boyfriend surprised us with a few gifts. Even though she tried to do what she could, it didn't stop my brother from releasing his mounting frustration. My brother was a teenager and started to openly express his internal anger towards our mother. She'd spank him but that didn't change or affect him one bit. To the contrary, it only made him angrier and he began to test her even more out of resentment.

Within a three-month time frame, during our first summer there, we had two fires in two different apartments. My mother claimed my brother was the cause of one of the fires and punched him in his chest so hard that he almost hit her back. He ran away after that incident and later returned with our uncle George to move out. My mother defended her actions and argued with my uncle over the situation while my brother went into our room and packed his things without giving me so much as a glance. He left without saying one word to me. My brother and I were the best of friends until we moved to Louisville. His moving out strained our relationship and filtered into our lives causing further separation from that point.

When my brother left I felt more alone than I could have imagined. My mother started to make reckless choices that I never thought she would. She was changing. She dated men who didn't really care for her and many times they had constant bouts of verbal abuse towards one another. If they weren't able to handle her, she found a way to manipulate them. I recall my mother dating a man who was a nice guy but when he tried to get too close she dumped him. One guy bought me a bike and two weeks later, when they broke up, he took it back. At that time, I thought it was funny to see how my mother was able to exploit some men, but when my father came around she was like a lost little girl.

At that age, I wasn't able to say or do anything to help the situation and once my father came back into the picture, things quickly changed for the worse. My parents argued all the time as if it were their normal routine. He'd come to our apartment and tell my mother to stop spending so much of his money and she'd retort by yelling at him about bringing marijuana into our home. Their arguments were so intense and frequent that they'd often instruct me to leave just so they could yell more. It was obvious that despite the fact that they loved each other they couldn't agree on anything.

The last time I saw my father during my childhood was one of the worst memories of him. My father and his best friend, whom I'll call Kane, came by the apartment one night. I was eating dinner and my mother was placidly watching television. My father told Kane to take me to the store and get some cigarettes. I hadn't finished eating but my father gave me a terrifying look that could kill, so I got up. My obedience towards my father had nothing to do with respect. Out of fear alone it wouldn't cross my mind to disobey him, so I left. When we returned I could hear the escalated voices of my parents arguing. Kane made me stand in the hallway and calmly wait for them to finish. I was angry with him because he acted as though it was okay for my parents to fight. Interrupting their voices was the startling sound of two gunshots. I knew they were gunshots from the similar sounds that blared out in my neighborhood but I'd never heard anything so well-defined, loud and chilling. I tried to force my way inside, but Kane physically restrained me from doing so.

For a brief moment, I stood shaking in complete terror as my father walked out of the apartment clutching his right arm. He gave me a blank stare and handed the gun to Kane. After Kane released me from his grip I rushed through the door to find my mother lying on her side with her hands covering her face. Full of unfathomable apprehension, I took very slow steps over to her, afraid that she wasn't going to move again. I bent down and sat next to her carefully trying to see if she was alive. Her body nervously jumped from the slight touch of my hand and I pulled her up to find her swollen eye turning into a deep violet color and her mouth bloody. Although she was badly beaten, I was grateful that my mother was alive.

Her body began shaking uncontrollably. She told me that she wished she hadn't missed, and had killed him! I was shocked at what I was hearing. I couldn't believe it! My mother intentionally tried to kill my father and then he beat her like a punching bag. My mother and I were traumatized over the situation. It took several days before we were able to talk about what happened. That was the last time I'd see my father for nearly twenty years.

LIFE: I've seen how a man is able to lead a woman down a dark and narrowing path that they should never take. Yet, once a woman believes it to be for *love* they go freely. Unfortunately, the path my mother chose to travel was crowded with lies, verbal, and physical abuse. Women have given men too much power for far too long. A woman will give her mind, offer her body, and open her spirit to a man she loves without hesitating to leave herself open to widespread neglect. Women can't help being emotional because their heart was made to love and that is all many of them know. A woman will forgive a man's wrongdoing and still love him unconditionally. But once her heart starts to hurt, so does her mind, and when her mind goes that's the point everyone around her begins to feel it or suffer in some way. Most women try to justify their faults by using the way men treat them as an excuse after they've neglected there own intuition for the love of a man. When a woman becomes broken she will allow her personal appearance to follow her broken spirit. Some of the responsibilities that were once important become neglected and burdensome. Most of all, a woman will ignore those that truly mean the most to her and often abandon her faith along the way.

There were several problems my mother had difficulty dealing with. One of which was created because of her desire to love and value the opinion that other people had of her more than she loved and valued herself. It may appear that pleasing others will get you what you want but in actuality, the person you're working to please may simply be using you. Take a look at their actions and determine what it is that they really want from you before investing in their madness. In an unhealthy way you may try to rationalize your decisions thinking they will make you happy. When you're left with nothing other than your own thoughts, lies, and lonely life you'll see what mattered the most. Having constant evolution, faith, peace, and happiness inside of you is priceless. Those things will bring other significant components to the surface. I watched the sweetest lady in the world turn into the toughest woman because of the choices she made. Her acceptance of abuse from a man gripped her and dragged her down like quicksand. The way she chose to align herself with life, for short-term gratification, was detrimental to her downfall. Take time to invest and find yourself before you lose yourself!

* * *

Chapter 3

THE BALL DOESN'T ALWAYS BOUNCE

I started to enjoy playing sports as a way to try and find peace but it didn't turn out that way. I realized that I was dropped in the middle of a jungle, which had now become my life. Although there was a Police Precinct sitting in the middle of the public housing neighborhoods, it wasn't safe.

Whenever I left the apartment I'd guardedly walk past the drug dealers who had the nicest cars, flashy clothing, and all the money they wanted. I saw guys gambling in plain view and some of them were barely my age. All of this was a typical scene in the neighborhood but the only problem was that I had to walk through it every single day to get to the outdoor basketball courts and recreational center. The temptation was always present, for many reasons, but there was innately something about gambling with my life that didn't sit well with me. I just wanted to be in a quiet zone for a change. I needed to find a place that could offer solitude if only for a little while. The basketball court was the one place I didn't have to see my mother or any of her bad habits. I didn't have to wonder if my father would randomly show up to render a beating to my mother until her eyes were swollen shut and she couldn't see. It was a place that I could actually be in control of my own life even if it was for merely a small fraction of time. No one has ever found their way without having the gift of being alone for reasons of self-discovery first.

The enticement to do harmful and negative things as a temporary means of surviving just never fit with what I believed would work for me. There were times I really needed help but after encountering a specific situation, I never thought twice about it.

There was a guy only a few years older than me named Jesse. He had two nice cars, a lot of clothing, fancy shoes, and flashy jewelry. It was part of his personality to show-off and he definitely made it a point to do so every time I saw him. Jesse polished his car while blasting his radio so you couldn't miss him if you tried. It seemed like some days he'd spend the entire day wiping his car down. It was funny watching him ride around because he still didn't have a driver's license. He would always speak to me and was cool with everyone in the neighborhood; at least that's what I thought.

One evening as I walked home from the basketball courts I saw Jesse's car lights on and his door hanging open. I was less than a block away and could hear a young girl frantically screaming for help. As I got closer, I saw his family run outside to his car. As I stared in shock, they were screaming and crying. It was terrible! He had been handcuffed to the steering wheel and shot multiple times in his head and body. Blood was everywhere and no one tried to move him. In fact, they didn't even touch Jesse. I saw everything very clearly, but I kept walking. It was a gruesome site, especially up close.

Just a short time after his death I saw his brother get arrested for selling drugs. Soon after that, the police raided their mother's home and had his entire family lying on the ground. They even arrested his mother. I told myself that I'd never do what those guys did because I knew that lifestyle wasn't the right way out of Peyton Place but it was unquestionably a way to die or end up in prison. It's easier said than done when you have very little and need a whole lot. However, to understand what you need to do, you must first understand what *not* to do. I decided to lay out my own plans of being something more than what I was used to seeing. The best thing about that was it was my decision to say *no* to the quick way out and hold onto my new dream of making it out.

LIFE: I was listening to a sermon one day and I heard a profound example of how many people have more to offer than they know. The story was about a drug dealer who complained about not being qualified to work in society. He explained that he had just completed a twenty-five year jail sentence. When asked about working at a restaurant as a manager he complained about how he wasn't qualified to do that job. The pastor asked him how he got to the top of his drug career. Without hesitation he began telling his story with confidence. He said he started off as a runner for a local dealer and after a few months he was able to get a direct line with the dealer. After a few more months, he became the main lookout for the dealer. Within a year, he was able to have his own corner to control. It only took him eighteen months to become the kingpin of his neighborhood. He spoke so proudly as he reflected on what he thought was a good life at the young age of eighteen.

The pastor kindly broke things down in a way that the former drug dealer would understand. If you were a runner for a few months, then you could have worked at McDonalds. If it only took you months to move up, surely you could have moved up to the cashier position. If it took you a year to get your own corner, then you could've been a manager in a year. If you were the kingpin in less than two-years, then you could've been an owner of your own restaurant in the same amount of time. The former drug dealer laughed and replied, "I don't know the first thing about running a business so I doubt that would work." The pastor smiled and gave him a life lesson beneficial to everyone. If you were able to sell drugs that means you know how to market a product. That's called Marketing. If you know how to get the word out that you're selling drugs that is called Advertising. If you're able to take care of your customers that's Customer Service. You have to know who to sell to and who not to sell to and that's called being a smart Manager. If you're able to sell drugs you're able to run your own legal business and still be the kingpin of your company, but you have to do it working just as hard as you did selling drugs. Staying up all through the night in any kind of weather while never making excuses to quit working proved you have the drive.

That man became the manager of a shipping warehouse and makes seventy thousand dollars a year. The message is, if we take time to learn we will be able to do whatever it is we choose to do. The choices you make are the choices that you live with!

* * *

Chapter 4

BASKETBALL BECAME MY FAMILY

My middle school was directly across from our housing project and the railroad tracks were the only thing that separated our apartment and my school. I'd begun to play basketball as part of my daily routine to avoid being at home. I practiced every day with my summer league coach, Chucky. He was the neighborhood coach for every sport and that was the best place for me to go when my mother started drinking heavily. My childhood friend Maurice Morris pushed me to play for our middle school team even though I was in the sixth grade. He was the star player and his nickname was, "Killer." He was built like an adult and his looks scared most people from wanting to guard him. He noticed how hard I played in pick-up games and asked me to tryout. I didn't want to be at home and I didn't have anything else to do, so I tried out for the team. Hildred Fisher picked me to join the team at DuValle Middle School! He made sure we all had acceptable grades before selecting his team.

Although my grades needed improvement being on the team would challenge me to do better.

After making the team I raced home to tell my mother the good news but instead I walked into our apartment to find empty alcohol and beer bottles all over the place. It was five o'clock in the afternoon and evident she'd been drinking heavily. I walked over to her in an attempt to tell her that I made the team but it was useless. The barely audible words that escaped her mouth were extremely slurred, making it impossible to understand anything she said. My heart dropped and a wave of disappointment covered my face. I ventured into my room, laid out my jerseys, and stared out the window despondently.

It's remarkable what a person remembers the most. That dark moment would turn into the brightest light that I could ever imagine but until then my darkness remained relatively dense for a while.

I began waking up at five o'clock in the morning to walk to the courts with my books tucked under one arm and my basketball in the other. I played basketball until it was time to catch the bus to school. My mind was laden with random thoughts that ran through my head. While shooting free throws I'd fantasize about having both parents around and being a close family. Whenever I'd shoot a free throw I'd stand at the line, correct my posture, and whisper while dribbling the ball three times, "One for mom, two for dad, and three for me," and then with a surge of confidence, I'd shoot the ball. The amazing part was I'd make at least eight out of ten, and sometimes, all ten. Nevertheless, reality reigned and I knew the thought of having my parents together was harder than the possibility of me making a hundred free throws in a row! Still, I remained relentless when it came to practicing my free throw. Literally, I'd stand right behind the line and shoot a ton of them until it was time to catch the bus to school. My environment wasn't the best but I finally created a routine that removed my focus from the negative things that were taking place in my life. Basketball gave me somewhat of a reprieve to focus on the only positive thing I really had.

At the age of eleven I arrived home from school on a Friday afternoon to find my mother gone. Since I didn't have a key and my mother had a new evening job, I assumed she'd be home a little later. Since she worked late I tried to knock softly to avoid upsetting her. She didn't answer the soft knocks so I was forced to knock louder. Still, no answer but I kept trying because she knew I'd be home by three. After a while I just left my books in front of the door and went to play basketball. I returned right before the streetlights came on because anything past that was unacceptable to my mother. I gave a soft knock first and then it got a little harder but when that didn't work I began pounding as hard as possible with my fist. After I stood by the door for five minutes hoping she'd let me in, I began kicking the door out of total frustration. Once I calmed down, my eyes caught sight of the large footprints I left on the door and it made me think. I sat on the steps and pulled out a pen along with a piece of paper and began writing about how I wanted things to be when I grew up. Those optimistic thoughts gave me my first glance at hope. They evolved from negative situations but allowed me to believe I could shape my own future.

I wrote about how I envisioned my life as an adult and my mind wandered freely into a creative place. I described where I'd live and defined the type of adult I'd be. Entertaining the thought of how differently I'd shape my life as an adult was great until I found myself waking up in front of my apartment door, with birds chirping. My mother still hadn't come home. I had a with a painful aching in my stomach that was making me sick so I gathered my things and hurried straight to my best friend's house. Terrance was always there for me. Sometimes God places people in your life to be there when the people that you expect to be aren't.

My best friend, Terrance Steward played football. He was an average height but physically built and he helped me sustain my strength and focus on who I was as a person, regardless of the way I acted, dressed, or spoke when something was wrong. Terrance remained a true friend to not only me but to everyone that meant well by us.

Terrance and his mother, Ms. Mary treated me like family and allowed me to eat with them without ever judging me in any manner. We often went to the basketball courts and played pick-up games all day. It was like having my brother back in my life and I had someone to lean on. We'd talk outside his apartment for a while before I'd decide to go home and see if my mother was there. However, I'd return to Terrance's wearing the standard look of disappointment on my face. Being locked out became routine and after a series of knocks and kicks on the door, I realized that I had to fend for myself and find something to eat, yet again. I had friends that I probably could've asked, but what kid goes over to another kids house and says, "Hey, my mom didn't come home last night, I slept in my hallway, and oh by the way, can I get some food because I don't know if I'll eat again tonight?" Instead of worrying or waiting on my mother, I decided to go to the grocery store because my friend Rodney worked there. He said he carried people's grocery bags to their car for money.

When I arrived I didn't see Rodney so I sat on the bench and watched people go in the store and exit with lots of bags. I was trying to grasp how my friend was able to make money when it looked like they didn't need any help. Suddenly, it hit me. If I catch them before they go in and ask if they need help then maybe I'll earn their business. I approached a nice middle-aged lady with a positive attitude and asked if I could help her with her groceries. She replied, "I don't need help shopping for groceries." It didn't take long before I realized I hadn't asked the right way and I needed to be a bit more aggressive with catching people. An older lady was headed my way so I asked very politely if I could help carry her groceries. She smiled, and with the sweetest voice replied, "Sure Doll." I waited outside for this lady to finish her shopping and when she came out carrying two bags, I immediately grabbed them and walked her to her car. After I put them on her backseat she smiled and with the sweetest voice said, "Thank you Doll, have a good day," and drove off! It's funny now, but when she drove off, I wanted to chase her down and jump on her hood. It hit me once again. I had to be polite with the introduction, explain what I wanted to do, and then tell them what I needed in return. The change in my approach was successful and I started to earn people's business along with their trust.

LIFE: Having a respectful introduction before you meet someone is always best. My first experience was asking people as they entered the grocery store if I could carry their bags to their car when they finished shopping. The chance of them having loose change coming out of the store was very high but most people were nervous about a young teenager hanging around the parking lot. I understood their perspective, however my kindness is what removed their fear. If they said *no*, my reply was still kind as some people only had a single bag and didn't need my help. Surprisingly, there were people that handed me some change because they observed how I carried myself. My actions left them with a positive impression of me and it didn't take long before I had regular customers. I didn't have a job, so I created one.

Don't allow your attitude to scare people away because once a person gets used to seeing you in a certain way that's how they will judge your character, good or bad.

I was so focused on working that I didn't notice it was getting late and I hadn't eaten in hours. Then, it struck me. I thought I made enough to get Kentucky Fried Chicken! I was excited until I walked into the restaurant and saw their prices. I made an immediate u-turn and headed back to the grocery store to buy a pack of bologna and a loaf of bread.

I took a negative situation and turned it into a positive one to help me survive. I had enough money to buy Kentucky Fried Chicken but I would've been broke again and hungry before the next morning. Since I was already accustomed to eating bologna sandwiches three times a week I knew it would last a lot longer than a nice, juicy, three-piece with a biscuit and mashed potatoes. At that time, it was a difficult decision because I had to learn how to survive on my own. It's funny, but reality has a way of making choices easier when the choices are limited.

I returned home and knocked loudly on my apartment door but again, my mother wasn't home. Once I realized she wasn't going to answer the door I got myself situated and opted to make my meal and write through the evening. In the middle of the night I was awaken by loud music and a crowd of people going in and out of my neighbor's apartment. I slid closer to my door as people walked past me going into what seemed to be a party. I wasn't embarrassed until one person asked another, "Wasn't he out here last night?" Hearing that comment alone caused me to look at my reality and I felt a great deal of suppressed anger towards my mother rushing to the surface. It was so great that I didn't care if she came home. Another wave of hurt struck me as I wondered why no one offered to help when they saw me sitting outside my door. I grabbed my things and headed to the park because I was certain it would be abandoned in the middle of the night. I sat my things down and rested on the bench as I looked up at the sky. I had never known how beautiful the stars were until that night. As I laid there I began reflecting on the drastic changes that were encompassing my life, which eventually led me to many unanswered questions. I couldn't understand why I was going through this when my brother was safe and happy. Why did an eleven-year-old kid have to endure what most grown men can't survive? Why couldn't my parents just love me enough to care for me? This was my reality. One thing I remember about that night was that although I was sleeping outside, I felt a sense of peace. I was alone but I wasn't scared to be by myself. I had just built another piece of armor for protection.

It was early Sunday morning and I woke up to the sound of two older men shouting at one another while playing basketball. I didn't realize I'd slept that late. I gathered my things while they completely disregarded me as though I was invisible to them and headed back home. As I approached the door I heard the television on inside our apartment. I walked in and saw my mother lying on the couch asleep. I glanced around the room and noticed her clothes scattered about, along with cigarettes and money on the table. I walked past her feeling sorry because she looked like she had a long night. Instead of emitting anger towards her, I knew I had to fill my heart and mind with something positive. I grabbed a blanket, covered her up, and then headed to the kitchen to make a sandwich. After eating, I cleaned up, then went back into the living area and laid right next to her on the floor so she couldn't leave without me knowing. I came to understand that I could survive on my own so my anger subsided since I knew my mother was okay.

When she finally woke up she went into the kitchen to make hot dogs and pork and beans, which was my favorite meal at the time. She never asked where I was, where I slept, or if I was okay mentally or physically. There was a natural separation progressing between us and I couldn't understand why my mother never expressed concern. I wondered what prevented her from showing that she cared about me.

Days went by and it didn't take long before I came home to minimal communication with my mother. She stayed in a somber mood. When she came home with her boyfriend she'd make me go outside so they could have the apartment to themselves. Our relationship evolved to me going into the apartment and immediately leaving without either of us saying two words to one another. She wouldn't ask where I was going and I wouldn't say where I was headed. It was the worst separation from my mother I've ever had. I felt as if she had no worries about what I did or how I lived anymore. I couldn't really show it or explain it to her, but my heart ached.

* * *

Chapter 5

MISTAKE AND EXCUSE
ARE JUST SPELLED DIFFERENT

The strained relationship between my mother and I carried on for over a year as I continued to find my solace and sanity in playing basketball. I was in the 7th grade and quickly became a better basketball player. The relief of playing basketball had given me the confidence I longed for and a bit of happiness that I craved.

My middle school team was considered to be the best in the area. We were known to have the only middle school players that were dunking in the games. I was a point guard and the other great players who would go on to play in college were, Maurice Morris who attended Southern Mississippi, Jermaine Brown attended the University of Tennessee and Georgetown College, Wardell Smith attended a junior college and Chris Travis attended Campbellsville College. We were a dominating team and it showed in our first game as we had 7 dunks and scored 92 points.

After having a great game and playing well, I arrived home to find that our apartment had been broken into and my mother was extremely upset. I knew she wasn't going to be in the best of moods so I dropped off my books, grabbed my basketball, and went to the basketball court to relive that night's game. I wasn't able to dunk as of yet but I wanted to so badly because my teammates were getting echoing cheers after they made their own thundering dunks. I'd practice running the team and then go in for a dunk. I was getting close but continued to miss the entire night. I went home with blisters covering my hands from missing so many dunks. The next day, I could barely write. The season was going great and after a few extra nights of additional practice, I finally heard the loud cheers that I desired. I had stolen a pass and it was just the opposing player and I on a fast break. I picked up speed so I could outrun him and as my adrenaline kicked in so did my momentum! I leapt into the air off one leg and as the player jumped with me, I slammed the ball in and knocked the kid to the floor! The crowd was screaming wildly and my teammates joined in. I smiled so hard that you could see all my teeth. The excitement was so intense that I didn't notice I cut my finger on the rim. I remember my coach always telling me to hold my emotions in and never let people know you haven't been there before. I didn't make a big scene even though I wanted to scream and shout! *The game of basketball gave me something that I never felt in my home, a sense of pride.*

The season was going well and my home life was the same but my attitude changed regarding my perspective about life. Before the turmoil in my family, my parents had shown me how to be respectful by saying, "Yes, Sir," or "No, Ma'am." They made sure I knew how to respect my elders and to be respectful to everyone I met. Although I had a lot of hurt and anger built up, those qualities never left me.

My father was a military man and he made it mandatory that I make my bed every morning, clean the bathroom every evening, and always made sure that he never had to remind me to do my chores. If he did there would be a spanking to remind me. I hadn't seen my father in a couple of years but since that was already instilled in my mind, it wasn't hard to understand what my coaches or teachers were telling me, especially if I ever ventured off the right path of doing the right things.

LIFE: There comes a point when children begin to make decisions for themselves and with those decisions come the responsibility and repercussions of their actions. Infused into the outcome of the choices they make comes the determination of whether or not they will embrace a sense of happiness and take pride in their decisions. As children grow into their teenage years they understand the basic premise for knowing the difference between right and wrong in most situations. Regardless, life is still one very large lesson with unforeseen pitfalls of its own. Understand, that a child may become a mirror image of their parent. Take caution in knowing that parents can set the stage for their children to have a very painful, challenging, or short life based on things they learn from your parental behavior. Additionally, they can have the opposite if you choose, as a parent, to invest in them properly. If they arbitrarily go off the path, which at some point they may, make sure they have an innate sense of taking ownership for their actions and have faith they *can* make changes to better themselves. Even if you aren't the best parent and have made choices that are destructive to your home environment, take ownership. Regardless of what you teach them and how well you've done raising them, keep in mind that because they are children, they will always have to figure some things out the hard way.

I went through seventh grade without much change in my home life. By the time I entered the eighth grade I continued growing in size and mental toughness while flourishing as a standout basketball player. Still, I couldn't shake the negativity in my home. The days that I spent wandering around as a lost kid began to fade away as my life was now built around schoolwork and basketball. The only issue I had was trying to figure out how to maintain my focus and balance. On one hand my coaches and teachers were disciplining me, but at home I wasn't being taught any life skills or responsibilities.

When basketball season ended I was forced to go home after school. This cheated me out of having the healthy and necessary release from the stress I carried, which only basketball seemed to alleviate. It was too cold to play outside and the older kids had the neighborhood gym until later in the evening. I thought I'd try to find a creative outlet so I'd sit at home and write many of my imaginative thoughts down on paper. They were completely random because I'd watch everything on television from Transformers, Alfred Hitchcock, One Day At A Time, and Johnny Carson to Martial Arts movies such as, "The Five Deadly Venoms" and then fall asleep while watching Sanford and Son or Good Times. My mind was all over the place but as I started to write I forgot all about my home life. I'd literally forget every negative thing that was going on with me. My mind was expanding and I was becoming more peaceful just from separating my focus from all of the bad thoughts that tried to hold my attention. The creativity I was expressing was exciting.

LIFE: If we took an assessment of ourselves, I think we'd be astonished at how many talents we actually have. What stops you from doing whatever you want? People tend to make career choices based on their financial needs instead of thinking of becoming an entrepreneur and utilizing their creativity. Sure money helps, but at times it can become a distraction that blocks happiness.

The problem that impedes progression in people is what I call "IF" people. "IF" stands for Internal Fears, and that is something we all possess. The power in having internal fear is learning how to break free of it and "IF" people, are those that break through their fears. The best ideas people have are never executed because the lack of desire to learn, fear of believing it will work, and holding onto anger about something in the past that you can't change. However, you can shape your future. Some of the most successful people didn't have a college degree before they became successful. Bill Gates dropped out of school to pursue his dream of starting Microsoft. Steve Jobs dropped out of college to work on learning how to create the MAC computer. Mark Zuckerberg left Harvard to launch Facebook. I don't encourage anyone to drop out of college but when you have a dream, make sure you act on it and not die with it!

Finding ways to become happy when I thought I had nothing to be happy about was a great feeling for me. I'd find a basketball court and go shoot hoops for hours on end, which often led into the late night hours. There were occasions I was upset about certain things and I'd stay out extremely late just to see if my mother would notice. I wanted her to become upset with me to prove she cared, but she didn't. Most nights, she was just arriving when I finally came home.

After months of living without parental supervision, I attempted to make adult decisions while thinking like a child. One day I woke up and noticed my mother hadn't come home again. I skipped school and stayed at home all day. When I was hungry I ate mayonnaise sandwiches, raw potatoes, and I made some powdered milk. Drinking powdered milk was like drinking paste, but when you're hungry and thirsty your taste buds go out of the window.

Things seemed bad but I didn't fully fathom that they could get worse until one day, while watching television our power went out in our apartment. I went outside and tried to see what happened but I had no idea the service was disconnected. I left the apartment and went to the playground to play basketball for a while. Later that day I returned home, the power was still off and there was no sign of my mother. I found a hall socket in the breezeway of my building so I took a lamp from our apartment, plugged it in and sat in the doorway writing until I grew sleepy. I woke up the next morning and again, my mother had not come home. It was a school day, but I figured I'd skip school again, watch television and eat sandwiches. Then, I remembered that I didn't have any power for television. The mayonnaise was hot and there wasn't any more bread to make sandwiches. Without power, I didn't have any way of knowing the exact time of day and was forced to get ready for school without knowing if I were early or late.

I called my girlfriend who lived a few miles from me and told her I missed the bus to school. She suggested that we stay home since we only had a few weeks left. We agreed and I walked over to her apartment. It was a bit odd because she was sixteen and I was thirteen. What was even more unbelievable was that her mother allowed us to stay together. Her mom was a sweet lady but I couldn't understand how she permitted two teenagers to sleep together and let me stay overnight for days at a time. It was strange, but I needed any help I could manage and being with her gave me a sense of happiness. I didn't worry if I'd have food to eat or a place to sleep. I felt like I had someone who cared about me.

I came home one day to pick up some of my clothes and saw my mother arguing with her boyfriend about him stealing money from her. I decided not to get involved and went to my room. I was so tired that I lit a candle, sat down, and began to write songs my girlfriend and I normally listened to. There were times that being in the dark didn't bother me because I didn't have to see the truth about where I was. My mother made a lot of excuses about things but I tried not to let them affect me. The excuses she made were nothing more than her inability to accept reality. I learned at an early age that no matter what, I *was* able to find a way to take care of myself, by myself.

The next day I walked out my room to find my mother gone and the place a wreck. I made the decision to stay home from school because I was angry with my mother. I waited all day for her to come home but again she was a no-show. After sitting around for most of the day, I jumped up and went to the basketball court. Later that day I returned to the same empty apartment. That night I decided to sleep on the couch so I could hear my mother when she came home, but she didn't so I kept the same routine the next day. I ended up missing school two days in a row.

The third day I went to school, but I went with a heavy heart and broken spirit.

I was standing in line for breakfast and another kid bumped into me as he entered the line to get his meal. When you're having a bad day anything is liable to happen. I knew I should have ignored it but my heart was in so much pain that I just pushed him as hard as I could. I watched him fall on the metal poles from where the lunch trays slide across and hit the floor. His body appeared lifeless. Because of the serious injury the kid sustained due to the fall, my principal thought I intentionally set out to hurt him. I didn't know how to respond so I acted as if I really didn't care what happened at that time. The principal asked me how to get in touch with my parents and I told him that I didn't know. He thought I was being rude, but it was the truth. He asked if I had anyone else he could contact to discuss what happened and again, I replied, "I have no one else to call and *no one* is going to help me." He thought I was being a jerk because my answers were dry and short so he called a police officer to take me to my mother. The officer took me home and when I turned the knob, the door was already unlocked. As we walked into my apartment I flicked the light switch; he noticed we didn't have any electricity. He told me to come with him and he took me straight to the juvenile detention center. I was told they had to keep me there until they were able to locate someone that could identify me.

The secretary asked a series of questions just as the principal had and I gave her the same flat answers. She asked if I had someone to call and I told her *no*.

She detected my attitude and warned me that the place I was being held wasn't a good place to be. My response to her was, "And neither is my house." While studying the details of my face she asked, "Who do you call when you need help?" She focused on my brown eyes that were beginning to show a trace of fear at the thought of her question. My voice was less angry and my tone became despondent as I replied, "God." I could tell by the look on her face that she felt sorry for me. I lowered my head and stared at the tiles on the floor. She told me she would get a bed for me to sleep on until they located my parents. I sat down and started to read the brochure about their program and it said I'd get three meals a day, two hours of exercise, and have the opportunity to work on a hobby. In my mind I thought I was getting a mini vacation! This was like being in paradise in comparison to the way I lived. Then, she explained that I would only be there for a short period of time because I had to go to a shelter. I was still happy because only a few nights ago I slept on a hard wooden bench and when I was able to get inside the apartment, there wasn't any heat or electricity.

It was my first night at the shelter and my roommate sat up all night complaining about the rules and how bad the food tasted. I wanted to tell that guy to shut up and be thankful he had a bed, some food, and working lights! Instead, I listened to him long enough to realize that people never know how good they have it.

I was at the shelter for a few days when I started to wonder if I was going to be adopted or put in some kind of boys home. I started thinking about why I was dealt a harsh blow at such a young age. I began to lose hope with each passing day, especially when I walked past the secretary's desk and she never called my name to leave. What I thought would have been a better situation became a miserable one and on top of that, my unappreciative roommate had both his parents come get him. I started to see other kids leave while I walked around the shelter home like it was my own house. I had a room to myself so I'd sit and write songs about my life. It was a good distraction because it was difficult when I thought about my reality.

I was sneaking across to the vending machine because I learned how to slide my skinny arm inside it and grab some chips. As I walked back to my room I overheard the secretary and her assistant talking. The assistant asked if she heard from my parents. The secretary told her, "No," and added, "No one has even called." The assistant stated, *"I'd be surprised if he makes it after he leaves here."* That comment would stay etched in my head, forever.

I went to my room, fell to my knees, leaned over my bed, and began to cry from years of deep-rooted pain and incessant loneliness. The pain struck my core because I hadn't felt the warmth of my mother's hugs nor the love from my father's presence. The memory alone brings about a sharp emotional jolt that I can't seem to shake. I tried with everything in me to make them proud of me but to no avail and to no reward of love from either parent.

I started to think about what I could do to prove the assistant wrong. I didn't know how to pray although I tried, and I knew nothing about Bible verses. However, I do recall praying that night because from that night on I'd always say my grace as a reminder to constantly thank God. I told God that if He let me out of that place I'd prove her wrong. That wasn't an angry or selfish prayer but a prayer asking God for an opportunity for me to make something of myself. I promised God when I made it I would do anything He asked of me. Most people want things to be given to them but I only wanted a chance to make my own decisions about my own life and shape my future.

LIFE: I hear the constant grumbling from kids stating that they allegedly don't have anything. Their inability to reflect on what they do have seems to be dissipating in this society and we need to help change that viewpoint.

One afternoon, I was in the mall having lunch with my son and one of his friend's. The young man was wearing a pair of Jordan sneakers, had a cellular phone, and an IPad while complaining about how he wished he had more. I asked the young man who paid for his items? He replied, "My dad bought my sneakers but I wanted a different pair. My grandmother bought my cell phone because my mom said she would only get me the Ipad." I didn't say anything. I just smirked and stared at the young man for a few seconds. He looked at my son and then back at me realizing what he said. He smiled and replied, "I should be thankful, huh?" I nodded in agreement. He got the point. I explained to him that material things don't show unconditional love but showing respect and appreciation for each other does. I communicated that his parents don't have to give him anything materialistic because their love will be there a lot longer than the gifts. He understood that he needed to change. He got up and went into a card shop and bought his parents, grandparents, and me a thank you card. I was impressed but sat him down again and told him, "It isn't the gifts that matter, it's your love that does." He looked a little confused so I asked him one final question. "When was the last time you told your parents or anyone you care about that you love them?" He said, "I don't remember." My retort was, "And neither do they." The most important gift you can give a child or parent is *love*. My children and I say or text, *I love you* at least once a day. It's better to know for certain than to wonder if someone is thinking of you or *if* they love you.

* * *

Chapter 6

IT TAKES A TEAM
TO MAKE A DREAM

My prayers were answered when a Doss High School assistant coach by the name of Bill White came to the shelter to speak to me. Coach White was a stern; yet fair man that was somewhat of a jokester. He offered me a new chance at life by helping me find my uncle so that he could sign me out of the shelter. He told me that the high school would help if I'd do the right things and stay out of trouble. He taught me a valuable lesson when I first met him and it was a painful one that I've held onto. After he offered to help me he shook my hand and then squeezed it so hard that I dropped to my knees. I thought this man was crazy because it was the first time we had ever met. He forced me to pay attention to him by squeezing the circulation out of my hand. He said something that every young man should know and practice until it becomes a natural part of their behavior. With a solid and stern look he explained, when you get respect you should always give that same respect in return. He said that only a real man would give respect first as he wants to be respected. That lesson about life made complete sense to me even at that age. Now, the pain I felt lasted a while so when he said it, I felt it even longer.

My uncle Maurice, who was my father's brother, picked me up from the shelter, which caught me off guard. I was waiting on my uncle George to appear but Coach White knew Maurice from a mutual friend. I was happy to see him but shocked because he and I had barely ever spoken. He was extremely understanding of my situation but never knew what I'd been going through. He drove me to my mother's apartment and as we walked up the stairs we noticed the door was already open which was an indication to me, the electricity was still off. My mother greeted me like I ran away. "Where have you been?" she shouted angrily. We went inside and Maurice had a talk with my mother sharing what happened. He directed his attention to me and said I needed to straighten up. I never said a word to my uncle Maurice about our living conditions because my mother was always ready to express herself, by any means necessary.

The situation was resolved. My uncle gave me five dollars and left without ever knowing how desperately I needed guidance. My mother started yelling at me for fighting and as I stood there with a blank stare, her hand flew onto the side of my face for not answering her. I learned to block out the screaming but in doing so I ignored her questions. The slap didn't hurt as much as the anger I felt from the past few days so I came out of my trance and headed to my room.

When I entered my room I realized my bed was gone and all I had was a mattress. That didn't bother me because I was becoming immune to my situation. While sitting in my room, I had visions of running away and trying to find someone to help me. But I remembered my shelter home roommate had run away and he ended up in the same place I was. I told myself that if I started running now, I'd never stop and I wouldn't be able to enjoy what peace I did have in playing basketball.

That night I looked out of my bedroom window for hours. After my body became weary I laid on the mattress and stared at the only thing illuminating the room, the candle. I watched it flicker until it went out.

Early the next morning I got up when the sun was beginning its ascent. I could see light coming through my room and something in me told me to get up and leave. I put my clothes back on, grabbed my toothbrush, notebook, and my beat up Optimus Prime Transformer toy that I got from the shelter home. As I walked through my living area I saw my mother sleeping on the couch with her boyfriend. I slowly shook my head and left.

After a while I didn't know what I was doing because I found myself walking towards the rising sun as if I could walk right into it. All I wanted was a little piece of mind and after I calmed down I decided to visit my mother's best friend, Janice. Janice's lived in Southwick. Even though it was still in the low-income housing area, I felt safe there. As soon as I gathered the courage to knock on her door, she opened it. Janice was surprised to see me and said she was headed to the grocery store. Before I could explain why I was there, she grabbed my shoulder and walked me inside her apartment. We began to talk and I told her what was going on with my mother and that I needed help. The conversation was so sincere that I walked with her to the grocery store. I actually enjoyed myself because I felt like a child who was talking with his mother. I felt at peace until we returned to her apartment to find my mother sitting on the porch looking very upset. I stopped dead in my tracks. I wasn't afraid of being spanked; I didn't want to go back home.

When we reached the porch, my mother didn't explode. Surprising to both Janice and I, my mother simply asked for money. I took the groceries inside while my mother stood outside and continued talking with Janice. Moments later, as I continued to unpacked the groceries; Janice entered the kitchen and began helping me. I looked at her and she gave me a disappointing smirk. I blocked my emotions from coming out and continued to act as if my heart wasn't hurting again.

The day was coming to an end and I didn't have any intentions on going back to my mother's apartment but Janice told me that she'd walk me home to make sure everything was fine. Reluctantly, I grabbed my things and headed out the door. When we arrived at my apartment we saw my mother and her boyfriend sitting outside of the building. Once she noticed that I was headed her way she got up and went inside the apartment. Without a word, her boyfriend left. Janice acknowledged my mother and then walked away. I followed my mother up the steps and she instructed me to wash the dishes. I asked her if we had any food and without warning she snatched ahold of my shirt, catching me off guard. She put her drink down and I pulled away from her and then took off running. There were at least eight steps between the door and me. Without thinking, I jumped down all of them! When she reached to grab me again I jumped so fast that she slipped and fell! I was so scared that I tore out of there, caught up with Janice, and told her what happened. I had enough of that situation and I finally begged her for help.

I was terrified that my mother was going to come over to Janice's house and give me a long butt whooping. But as the night went on, she never showed. I thought that either she hurt herself while trying to grab me or she was content on me not coming back home. Either way, I felt relieved because in the meantime, I was safe.

The next morning my uncle George pulled up to Janice's apartment looking very angry. We drove back to my mother's apartment so they could talk but as soon as we walked in an argument immediately ensued. I went back out to my uncle's car and waited for him. By the time he returned, he was clearly frustrated. He headed to his home and as he was driving he began talking to me about life. Twenty minutes later, we pulled up to an apartment in a nice middle class neighborhood. He continued to tell me how I needed to grow up and be a young man with character. He was strict but always upfront like my

57

great-grandmother. He treated me as his son and since he didn't have any children at the time, he allowed me to stay with him.

My uncle George was very intelligent and the first male in our family to graduate from college. He always made it a point to make sure I knew my history, where I came from, and what it meant to be a good person. I tried to settle under his roof but I found myself trying to do things my way because I was accustomed to doing so much on my own. I lived like I did while living with my mother. I'd stay at my girlfriend's house whenever I felt like it and I stayed out late playing basketball. He sat me down and told me that I couldn't act that way if I wanted him to help me. I didn't have a level head at that time so I made up a story and said I was going to stay with my mother when I actually went to stay with my girlfriend. I lived with her until the week before I started high school.

On my way to the bus stop I ran into my friend, Maurice Morris. He was at his stop, which was near the one I was supposed to get on. We began to talk about things and I became distracted. Without thinking, I climbed on the bus with him. When the bus arrived, I got off and walked into Fairdale High School and was amazed at how many of my middle school teammates were there. I followed the trail of kids going into the cafeteria for breakfast and headed towards the line, too. Suddenly, I felt a strong grip on my shoulder. I turned around and realized it was Coach Bill White. He escorted me out of the building and took me straight to Doss High School, where I'd been given an address so I could attend. It was my teammate's address that I was using and I began to stay with him in order to attend Doss.

My teammate was a senior at Doss and we shared some of the same issues. His mother was a heavy drinker and their relationship was challenging as well. We became good friends but after staying there for a while I could tell that I was becoming a burden. His mother began expressing her frustration about me staying over and it didn't take long before I soon found myself in an abysmal cycle of trying to find shelter. My life quickly spiraled downward.

I wandered from place to place trying to find a meal and a place to sleep. I stayed at three different teammates homes, my best friends, my girlfriend's, and I even stayed at Janice's sometimes. I was all over the place and everyone knew how I was living but no one did anything to help me find a place to settle down. I couldn't be upset because they weren't responsible for me, but having to figure it out on my own was difficult and disheartening.

LIFE: I was cognizant that the decisions I made were part of becoming an individual thinker as a young adult. When I heard some of the statements I made, and paid attention to the way I was thinking, I became aware that I was just another kid making excuses. It was imperative for me to change my way of thinking and not allow the dark environment I was in to shape my thoughts and regulate my decisions. It became that my parent's bad habits were something I didn't have the power to change. However, I could change my negative surroundings if I wanted to. Once I began to notice how passionately I fought to get out of each situation, I started to forgive myself and release some of my own anger. I wasn't going to blame others for my circumstances because it was unfair. Instead, I made a conscious decision to change my situation by changing my state of mind so I could do what I desired most.

People knew I was less fortunate and although I never had a weak mind, my spirit became weak and sometimes broken. The problem was, while some people were enjoying the sunshine I was constantly blocking mine. I've never been poor, only broke, because being poor is a disabling state of mind, and broke was the situation I was in at that moment.

When I say I was less fortunate I mean by way of opportunities in my personal life. I had to wear two pairs of socks to fit a size thirteen shoe when I actually wore an eleven. I wore my teammates pants that were usually two sizes too big and almost too short to wear because I was taller than he was. I carried around a small grocery bag with a toothbrush and deodorant inside. I didn't have much therefore, I taught myself how to sustain until I could make changes. When I didn't have a place to stay I went into survival mode. I'd visit other schoolmate's homes and pretend to fall asleep so I had a place to stay for the night.

There came a point when I ran out of options and remained in the inner city area most of my freshman year of high school. I made adjustments to survive but I didn't like what I had to do. I broke up with my girlfriend, stopped communicating with my uncle George, and basically ran out of excuses to stay at people's homes. I remember going to restaurants that served bread and water as a complimentary appetizer. I'd scarf down the bread and gulp my water as fast as possible and then tell the server that my parents were on their way. My other exit strategy was simple. When I was done, I'd tell the server that I was at the wrong place. Without another word, I'd get up and leave. I never considered it to be stealing because they couldn't charge me for something they gave away.

Out of pure necessity, I continued to establish ways to fend for myself instead of doing something I knew was going to hurt me or someone else. I saw the drug dealers in my neighborhood and wished I could have what they had but my best friend Terrance and I agreed that we'd never sell or use drugs because of the destruction it brought to our family members as well as to those that used them.

One of his family members got caught selling drugs and had to go to jail for a long time. My father sold drugs and it broke up our family. Although the image a drug dealer had appeared to be favorable, the reality behind that life was terrible. Watching what happened to my neighbor and his family left a vibrant picture in my head. I wasn't willing to sacrifice my life or freedom for short-term gratification. That was clearly a dead-end path.

My high school friend drove to school in a freshly painted Buick. It had nice, new rims coupled with a loud sound system inside. He'd go flying past us while we were on the school bus and smile as we admired his ride. That would all come to an abrupt halt, just like so many others that made the choice he had. We were leaving the basketball court heading down the hill to Terrance's apartment when we noticed his car whip around the corner going extremely fast. Behind him were a slew of police cars chasing him with flashing lights. We laughed and tried to catch up to the chase. We cut across the neighborhood following the sounds of the sirens because the neighborhood was one big maze. We raced through the entire neighborhood just to see if he'd gotten away, which we were hoping for, because he wasn't a bad guy. A few minutes later there was a loud sound of a collision! He crashed his car into one of the brick buildings and the police snatched him out of it and beat him. He didn't fight back but they violently punched and kicked him until he could barely stand, then they yanked his arms behind his back and handcuffed him. People were screaming towards the police but as we got closer we heard a few older ladies screaming at our friend. The expressions on their weary faces were undeniably pain-stricken but we didn't know why. We saw a huddle of people gathered closely together across the street and headed that way. When we reached the crowd someone told us that our friend hit a little girl while running from the police. We couldn't believe it. When I forced my slender body in between the thick crowd my mouth involuntarily fell open and my eyes widened. The shocking image was nauseating! In front of me was the body of a little girl. She couldn't have been more than eight-years-old although it was difficult to gauge. Her leg was dismembered and her head was smashed into the cement. Her young body was lying in a thick pool of bright red blood steadily gushing out of her. It was the worst sight I'd ever taken in!

A few days later, we found out that our friend was running from the police because he had a suspended license. They said he would have done a few months in jail but now he was going to prison for several years for killing the little girl.

After that, my friends and I played basketball and football throughout the year just so we could stick together and stay away from negative influences, temptations, or dangerous situations.

* * *

Chapter 7

BUILDING ENDURANCE

The basketball season was about to commence and the new assistant coach, Terrance Moorman, noticed my physical appearance and lack of attentiveness in my classes. It was impossible for me to stay awake when I was always on the hunt for a place to stay or a meal. I'd easily surrender to sleep in class, my clothes looked dirty and I wore many of the same outfits repetitively. One afternoon, Mr. Moorman pulled me aside to talk with me. I was waiting on another "I Have a Dream" speech but he gave me some shocking advice. He told me that regardless of what I was going through at home, to make sure I took care of myself first so I'd be able to change my situation. I had no idea what he meant but then he went deeper and said, "If you think someone will feel sorry for you when they have their own problems, then you will never be happy. Find a way to get yourself right. *Find a way!*" His powerful words stayed in the forefront of my mind and it started to make sense that day in practice.

I spent time working on a new basketball move and decided to try it in practice that day. I used it on my teammates. I slowed down on a fast break, did a spin move around my opponent, and then tried to dunk the ball. Everything went exactly how I planned it and the grand finale was when I dunked on our six-foot-six center. My coaches and teammates were in disbelief! We celebrated my athletic display and creative ingenuity while laughing hysterically. My coach, Leon Mudd, came into the huddle and asked what got into me. I replied, *"I just found a way."* Coach Moorman smiled and nodded in approval. Coach Moorman became my new basketball mentor when my uncle George wasn't around. He was a former Doss basketball player. He stayed after practice just to help me work on my game. He'd make me dribble a tennis ball up and down a flight of steps until I did it without looking down or losing the ball. Furthermore, he didn't allow me to leave until I made a hundred shots. It was fun and it taught me to discipline myself. One day after practice, I had such a great time perfecting my skills that I hadn't paid attention to how late it was. I raced down the stairs to change clothes and realized everyone was gone except the janitor. He took his keys out and let me into our locker room so I could get my clothes. I missed the bus and coach Moorman had just left. I went back to the gym, sat on the edge of the stage, and changed clothes. I slowly walked across the hardwood floor looking at the stars and I saw names such as Ernie Whitus, Brandy Monks, and Chip Watkins who were all state players. As I continued to walk around the gym I even noticed that we had a female player who won Miss Basketball in the state of

Kentucky named Kim Pehlke. I changed back into my basketball gear and returned to the court to work on our team plays. I challenged myself to play every position so I knew where each player on the court was supposed to be. I pretended to be better than all of my teammates. Since I knew how they played, I mastered each of their moves. It was my way of trying to beat them in practice the next day. I recall only taking breaks for water because I had nowhere to be or anywhere to go. I started walking around the gym and as I looked at the names and accomplishments of all those great players I saw who had the most points, assists, and even the wins. I imagined I broke every record and after making a great shot, I'd run around the gym celebrating as though I had a bunch of family and friends around cheering for me.

While taking a break from practicing, the janitor came in and told me he was cutting the lights off. He asked if I had a ride and I said, *yes*. I could tell he didn't believe me, but he said he'd leave one light on for me. It was a Friday and we had basketball practice on Saturday at ten in the morning so I decided to stay in the gym and get ready for the next day. I went to the back door and propped it open so I could get back and forth to the restroom. I was accustomed to sleeping in different places so it never bothered me when it was a new place. I went back into the gym, climbed on the back of the stage behind the curtains and laid there. I wasn't upset that I had nowhere to go because I was happy that I was becoming someone that I could be proud of.

The next morning Coach Moorman walked in, noticed that I still had the same clothes from the previous day, and walked out of the locker room expressionless. I had a great practice and when we were done he pulled me to the side and said, "I'm proud that you didn't make any excuses and that you stayed focused on getting better." His words of encouragement resonated with me because they were always positive. That little encouragement gave me a tremendous sense of self-pride and I was determined not to let anything or anyone stop me from being my best!

That weekend I received some good news. My mother's friend Janice found out where my mother was and took me to a run down building in a place called Old Louisville. It was an older area where mostly retired or elderly people lived. The building looked decrepit and appeared to have major structural damage and bad roofing. The steps were uneven from the way the ground had shifted and there were police everywhere. I waited to see what was going on and then I saw my mother's boyfriend being escorted out of the building. I was eager to see if my mother came out, but she didn't. Janice took me to the door and said in a hushed tone, "That's the door." I asked why she wasn't coming in but Janice didn't answer my question, in an alarming voice she stated, "She's in there." I disregard her wave of fear because I was excited to see my mother. I knocked on the door and she opened it screaming, "Now what do you jerks want?" she questioned, angrily. I started laughing because she thought I was the police but when she saw me she said, "Oh I thought you were somebody else." She was sweet and said, "Hey, boogie." It reminded me of living in Flint where we use to have fun and enjoyed being together.

I entered her dimly lit apartment to find broken glass and clothes thrown all over the floor; it was in shambles. I noticed my mother had gained a little weight. I asked how she was doing and without answering she asked how I knew where she lived. It didn't' take but a minute for reality to settle back in. I told her Janice found her for me and she rolled her eyes. I could tell she was upset so I tried to defuse the tension and began cleaning her dirty apartment. She didn't ask how I was doing or where I'd been, and surprisingly, it didn't bother me at all because I was merely excited to see her again. In an attempt to find out if she was okay, I initiated the conversation about what I witnessed before knocking on her door. She explained how her boyfriend had been stealing her money and said she was upset with him. I could tell that she was going through a lot so I continued to help her clean the apartment. I stayed with her for a couple of hours and when I got hungry I began to ask if there was anything to eat. Before I had a chance to finish my sentence, she snapped, "No, and I don't have any money." I knew the situation all to well so I made my way to the door. I told her I was leaving and I'd stop by and check on her from time to time and she said, "Okay." She walked into the kitchen, as I walked out of the door. I didn't know how she felt or what was going on so I acted like I'd see her another day. When I walked out of that apartment it felt as if my soul had been ripped from me. There's nothing like a mother's love, but *I promise you,* there is nothing worse than not feeling your mother's love!

The walk back to Janice's house was long and gave me time to think. When I got there she looked sad. I asked her why she didn't come inside with me and she told me she wasn't supposed to show me where my mother lived. I sat down and we began to talk more. Janice told me that my mother didn't want to see me. I held back my tears for about three seconds before realizing I couldn't fight them any longer. I cried with an uncontrolled surge of anger combined with years of hurt. Why would a mother make the choice not to see her son, let alone raise him? How was it possible for any mother to be so unloving? I couldn't image my life being this way and I didn't find it conceivable for us to ever have a sustainable relationship again. Janice tried to console me but I was so infuriated I stormed out of her house and went to the only place I found peace, the basketball court. It was cold outside but I took off my jacket, tossed it on a bench and started playing basketball. This time, my uncontrolled anger wouldn't allow me to focus. I grabbed the rim and pulled on the goal with all my strength, trying to break it off of the backboard. With every yank of the goal I felt everyone that pulled away from me. My reality was that I was alone in this world. Once my anger began to subside, I was willing to face the life that I was given. At that moment, I made a decision to find a better life and live it.

I had a lot of problems that I had to work through. I didn't have a home, or even my own clothes, which was embarrassing, but what hurt more was not having anyone know or care about where I was from day to day. Actually, it was more upsetting than sad. However, the biggest problem I had was *me*! I wasted a tremendous amount of energy trying to figure out why no one helped me. I expected that someone should care because I was a kid! Although I tried, I continually allowed my anger to impede my progress. That day, I decided I would stop comparing my life to someone else's. I'd never stolen anything to compensate for not having something. I didn't talk about people to get attention. I just couldn't grasp why I was so less fortunate than other less fortunate people. It's like a homeless person asking another homeless person for a place to stay. I had to find my way in life and it was a hard road, nonetheless it was the only road I had to go down.

LIFE: It's hard to know when your character develops into something strong and worth investing in but I believe this caused mine to finally reveal itself. Adversity made me stronger as it showed me what kind of person I was capable of becoming, if I wanted to. It didn't appear that life was naturally going to hand me a free golden ticket. Once I stopped expecting someone to help me, making excuses, and blaming my parents, *life and I* had a better understanding. I started to perceive my parents in a different way. They weren't bad people, they were people with bad habits that didn't have faith and refused to change. Acknowledging reality was a liberating experience. Their struggles made it easy for me to see what I didn't want to become. My focus was now, my journey.

* * *

Chapter 8

QUITTING IS NEVER AN OPTION

My freshman year was like a walking nightmare but by the time summer hit I was recognized as a top player in my region. Things didn't change too much except I made new friends, which offered opportunities for me to have a place to stay. I spent the summer keeping to the same routine I maintained during the school year, such as staying over friend's houses, playing basketball and carrying bags at the grocery store.

Up until that point, I hadn't thought about what I wanted to be until I visited a friend of mine, Tim. His older brother was cutting their lawn and I asked Tim why his brother had his work clothes on while he was cutting the grass. He told me that his brother owned his own lawn service and he was actually at work. I asked if he charged their parents to cut the grass and Tim said, *yes.* He told me that his parents said they would rather teach their son how to earn a decent pay instead of just giving him money. I asked if it was possible to work with his brother and he told me that

I'd have to be serious because his business was his livelihood. I agreed and went to work with him for two weeks before he told me that he couldn't use me anymore because he needed a full-time employee. After seeing my first weeks pay, I really thought deep and hard about staying with his company and quitting basketball. I asked him how much he would pay me if I became a full-time employee. Tim quickly cut me off and said, "Don't even think about not finishing school because you can cut grass forever but you only get one chance at getting a good education."

I understood him but I needed money and I had to take care of myself so I stayed diligent in finding ways to survive. I secured a few summer jobs such as delivering newspapers and washing cars. When I saved enough money I went to buy clothes at the Goodwill and since I'd grown taller I was hoping they'd have clothing that would fit. I was six-feet-four but weighed only one hundred and fifty pounds so finding clothes that fit me was a difficult task. I went to the store and tried my best to put things together but I made some bad selections that day. I wasn't used to having anything so I didn't know what size I needed. I bought long pants but the waist was entirely too big. I tried to buy some long sleeve shirts but the length was way too short. Ultimately, I found somewhat of a decent outfit to make an appearance at our city park festival.

It was the first day of the city park festival and I wore my basketball shoes from the previous year, a plaid pair of shorts, and a plaid shirt. I thought it matched well and felt I looked pretty cool. I went to the park and people were laughing and pointing at me. I met with some of my friends and they started joking on me too. I told them that I was just being silly and then I opened my shirt in hopes that it might break up the outfit but it didn't help. Without attracting any more attention than I already had, I disappeared and went to my uncle George's house since he lived nearby. I saw smoke rising from his backyard and followed the trail to find him grilling with some of his friends. My uncle couldn't help but to laugh at my outfit as he walked me inside his house.

We had a long talk and he asked if I needed anything. That's when I told him some of the things that I had been doing for the past year. I didn't tell him everything but I told him how badly I needed some guidance. It felt great to have someone to vent to. He allowed me to stay with him again and he took me school shopping. I felt that my life was about to change for the better.

LIFE: You won't begin to heal until you are willing to release your pain, forgive people in your life and begin to have faith. Sometimes you may have to do it alone. However, if you have someone you trust that will be honest enough to tell you the truth and perhaps help you through it, value that person. It doesn't mean they have to take care of you but if they are a positive influence listen to them and put their advice to use when warranted. Some people will tell you what you want to hear just to keep you as a friend. A real friend will have real conversations to help you develop into a better person and you shouldn't hesitate to return the favor.

***

Chapter 9

FATIGUE WILL MAKE OR BREAK YOU

I came home after practice feeling great. My life was going better and nothing could have shaken me up until the point my uncle George handed me a piece of paper without saying a word. I opened it and my mind couldn't comprehend what I was reading. It didn't make sense so I asked him, "What's child support? Is this for me?" He nodded his head and replied, "Yes. And it means you have to get a job to take care of your son." I looked back at the paper and it said I was the father of a child named after me. I was fourteen-years-old when I fathered a child! I dropped my head and was overcome with fear. With the example I had as a father, I was certain I didn't have a chance of being a good father to my child. However, my uncle George was going to make sure I could do it.

I got a job, stopped hanging out after practice, and worked weekends. I didn't know how to feel about having a son since I hadn't seen my father in years. I was scared to death because I didn't want him to go through the heartache and pain that I was working to break free of. I found my ex-girlfriend who I had lived with and tried to talk to her about what was going on. She told me she tried to find me when she was pregnant, but couldn't. I didn't believe her because I had been on the local news and she knew exactly where to send a letter. But I let my frustration towards her go so we could make plans to try and reconcile the relationship for the sake of our son. I agreed, but I still had to pay child support because she was receiving government aid like my mother had received.

After trying to find a good-paying job to take care of my son, I took a job on a candy truck across from my old neighborhood. The family who owned Whiteside's were really great people because not only did they make money from the neighborhood, they reinvested by helping people when they could. I worked at Whiteside's everyday after practice and then all day on Sunday's. I got bored easily because I wanted to hang out with my friends. I wanted to make more money so I asked the owner's son, Robert if I could take some candy to school to sell. He agreed so I set-up shop. During school hours, everyone came directly to me and I enjoyed feeling like a businessman. This gave me a sense of faith in my ability to take care of my son regardless of what job I worked.

My regular job at Whiteside's candy truck was to sell the candy, count the cash, neatly restock all of the candy and lock all the doors and windows. I was aware of my surroundings and took pride in making sure everything was in order. I followed the same routine every evening just like people that worked in my neighborhood. One night while leaving the candy truck, I saw three guys walking towards me. I recognized one of the guys from my neighborhood so I didn't pay them any attention. As we passed each other, I felt a yanking of my bag and a hard hit to the back of my head. Before I could turn around I felt another blow to the side of my face. Those punches had minimal affect on me because I was holding on to my candy for dear life. The guys held me down and began punching me, but I didn't bother to cover my face because all I kept thinking about was, "Please don't take my son's food!" After they realized I wasn't going to let go of the bag, one of them kicked me in my mouth and it felt like my tooth came out. I finally let go of the bag and rolled over to find blood streaming from my mouth. They took the candy and never once looked in my pockets to take my money. I only had two dollars but it was as if they knew how valuable the candy was to me. I was angry and felt violated so I went looking for those guys. It wasn't the smartest thing to do but when you're trying to provide for your child, the only thing that matters is not seeing his face of disappointment. I didn't ever want him to be hungry or to need anything. I wanted to take care of him and I needed to prove to myself that I could.

I used my shirt to stop my mouth from bleeding and continued looking for those guys. I ran into my cousin who was a known street guy and explained to him what happened. He told me he'd take care of it. He advised me to page him if I ever needed him and said he'd be there for me. I knew he was into the same business my father was in so I kept my distance from him as much as possible.

Before I knew it something else struck me really hard. It was common sense. I had to discipline myself before I went down a one-way street towards trouble. Although I wanted to get those guys back, I knew I had to continue to keep my life on track. I remembered what that lady said at the shelter about how I probably wouldn't make it and I still wanted to prove her wrong. I put another shield of armor on and it was a mask that came with a new temperament. My mask smiled and hid my pain. As long as people didn't think I was struggling with problems or carried a duffle bag full of grievances, they were willing to help me without knowing how much I needed help.

It was challenging to keep putting that mask on because at times, I felt like I was losing myself in the process. The thing about my mask was the fact that I could use it to keep going forward and not backwards. A great number of my friends put on the wrong mask and were going so far backwards that I never saw them again. They gave in to the very environment they should have been working to escape. Instead, temptation won. Some went to prison, many submitted to gang violence or drugs, while others died.

At the age of fifteen I was working to pay child support for my one-year-old son and I was keeping him over the weekends if I didn't have a basketball game. I was becoming a very good basketball player while still doing well in school and at home. But like my great-grandmother used to warn me, if you live long enough nothing will ever stay the same. I found that out in a burst of flames.

Things were getting tougher because I didn't have enough time in the day to accommodate my son.

After a while I began to take my son to work with me when I delivered newspapers on the weekend. A few weeks passed and my boss explained that it wasn't a safe environment for my son to be around and I was prohibited from taking him with me any longer. He'd sit in the backseat while I jumped out of the truck to throw papers in people's yard. He was in his car seat so I thought he was safe but the car seat was so old and used that my boss didn't agree with me. Things became increasingly difficult because I didn't have the solution yet. I wasn't going to stop spending time with my son because he was my primary reason to fight so hard. To keep my focus on my priorities I even changed my free throw routine from dribbling three times for my mother, father, and I to one dribble for my son and the second dribble for me. Just like my last routine, I made nearly all of my free throws.

For a short time, I still had one other job to keep things progressing. Subsequently, I found out that the owner was sick and wasn't able to keep the candy truck open. I was really feeling the pressure of an adult and I knew I was supposed to take care of my child because he was my responsibility. My girlfriend asked me to move in with her and said if I didn't she was going to break up with me again. I knew my uncle wouldn't allow that so I went through a teenage break-up, which felt like I was getting a divorce.

Shortly, after the breakup, I ran into my mother's friend, Janice while I was on my way to pick up my son. She told me that I needed to go see my mother and that it was urgent. I thought about going, but every time I saw her it was hard and I felt like I'd be disappointed again. Unfortunately, I didn't have a mask to help me handle that type of pain but knowing that my son was waiting encouraged me to stay focused. My mother's life was something I didn't have control over, nor could I change it, but I could help change my son's. I made the choice to be responsible and be with my son instead of repeating the cycle of chasing something that wasn't really there. I didn't see my mother that day.

I arrived at my girlfriends' apartment and when I got to the door there was no answer. I was early so I waited outside for a while. I went to a payphone and called her house phone but she didn't answer. It felt like I'd been waiting outside for several hours so I went back to her place and waited outside until the sun set. I had fallen asleep but woke up to my girlfriend walking a guy out of her apartment. I gave him a look but he didn't know what was going on so he spoke while I ignored him. She asked me why I was still sitting outside and I told her I was there to pick up my son. She told me he was asleep and to come back tomorrow. I put on one of my masks, but this mask was the angry one. We exchanged words that shouldn't have been spoken and because of them, we didn't see eye to eye ever again. She told me that I could never come around unless I spoke to her first. When I left I had to walk all the way to my uncle's house because I missed the last city bus. I was so upset that I didn't pay attention to the long walk home.

When I arrived at my uncle's house, he was livid because I'd awaken him before he had to be at his third shift job. He told me if I didn't straighten up I wouldn't be able to stay there anymore. It was already late, my uncle was unhappy, and then the phone rang. It was my cousin whom my uncle disliked because of his lifestyle.

My cousin told me that he saw my dad and asked if I wanted to talk to him. I thought about it but our last encounter popped in my mind so I told him, "No." He asked me if I was sure and I replied, "My father lives in the same city as I do and if he wanted to see me he would have done so by now. So, no, I don't want or need to see him." We hung up and even though I said, "*No,*" I really did want him to be around me. At the very at least, I wanted him to see how much I'd grown and to see his grandson. It was a long night and I usually pulled out the couch bed but I was so exhausted I turned on the television and started watching Sanford and Son. I fell asleep on the floor with the television still on.

I woke up the next morning and had forgotten about the day before. It was odd but it felt good because I wasn't upset. All I kept thinking about was how funny Sanford and Son was. I turned on the television and watched more episodes and it was as if I had no worries in the world. Having the ability to change my thought process made a huge difference. I understood that I could avoid being unhappy if I found out what actually made me happy.

LIFE: This is a simple format that not everyone grasps. If you have something that can provide you with peace of mind that isn't disrespectful to anyone including yourself, then enjoy that until you calm down. Laughter is often the perfect release. It will give you time to get your thoughts in a healthier place. You'll think more clearly as opposed to thinking out of hurt or anger. The best way to stay calm is to practice staying calm. Instead of throwing out anger, share positive thoughts when someone does something to disrupt your spirit.

"May all my enemies live long to see God bless me with happiness." The revenge we all crave at times should be channeled with a strong belief in forgiveness and seeking happiness.

* * *

Chapter 10

MISS OUT BEFORE YOU MESS UP

There are numerous occasions that we've done something and if the results weren't what we anticipated we end up uttering, "I knew I shouldn't have done that." The reason is because we didn't follow our intuition. Instinctively most people know better but ignore their opposing sense. Then there are times that you've been faced with the conscious decision to do something that challenges the very fiber of who you really are, meaning again, *you knew better*.

Before you react too quickly in any situation think about the repercussions then take it a few steps further and consider the worse thing that could happen if you made that choice. Irrespective of the outcome, because you didn't think it through, the consequences could be life altering. If you tell yourself that people will be hurt, your reputation permanently damaged, you'll end up in prison or dead, then make the choice to miss out before you mess-up.

I was in the process of making poor decisions simply by being around my cousin who was always doing things to make money. However, the majority of the things he did weren't legitimate and were considered dangerous. When I ran into him, he'd let me hang out with him and his friends. I started to lose focus on my personal development because he made things easier by giving me money to pay child support and provided me with clothes to wear. I started enjoying myself but I was conscious that I wanted a better life so I continuously kept my eye on what was going on around us.

I always had a strange feeling when I was with him. I felt that somehow I was a part of the negative activities he took part in solely through my association, but since I never did any of those things I felt like I wouldn't get into trouble. Therefore, I justified my hanging around him. It was a foolish thought that would eventually lead to foolish problems.

Late one night, my cousin and I pulled up to a house party. Before we could get out of the car, the sound of gunshots rang out, spraying his car with bullets. My cousin took a quick assessment of the environment, jumped out the car, and fearlessly headed towards the house. Vigilantly, my eyes followed his every move and I watched as he pulled out a gun and ran towards the side of the house. I got out because I felt obligated to help him because of everything he'd done for me. Then, I saw him running back towards me while firing shoots at someone. I jumped in the car but he ran past me and hid behind another parked car. I couldn't understand why he didn't jump in his car and drive away but then, I saw two guys appear from the side of the house and commence shooting towards my cousin. I ducked down as far as I could without loosing site of him. Finally, they ran towards the house while my cousin jumped in the car, and finally peeled off.

This was beyond what I conceptualized and I was shaken, but so was he as I watched him franticly pull out his large cell phone and call his friend in a panic. He asked me if I was okay and then dropped me off at my uncle's house. I was already nervous but I got even more worried when my uncle saw me get out of his car. When he noticed the new clothes I was wearing and my cousin's fancy car, either anger or disappointment covered his face. It may have been both.

My uncle George actually took time yet again, to warn me that all my decisions have consequences whether they are planned or unplanned. I heard him, and understood, but I knew I wasn't doing anything wrong and I felt my cousin was actually trying to help me handle my problems. My uncle disagreed and in return made some strict rules and timelines so that I'd have to straighten up or leave.

I listened, for about a week, and then I asked my cousin to pick me up for a big game I was having. I met him around the corner so my uncle wouldn't see me get in his car. He asked why I did that and I told him that my uncle didn't think I should hang with him and he became enraged. He spewed out a barrage of profanity explaining how he was just trying to help. I assured him that we were family and I wasn't going anywhere. He took it to heart but continued to vent. I understood his position because he never tried to pull me into doing anything that he did, but he was willing to take care of me because we were family. My cousin gave me my first twenty-dollar bill. I was so happy that I placed it in the bottom of my shoe just so I wouldn't lose it and no one would take it.

Shortly after that conversation we pulled up at my high school gym and some of my classmates saw me get out of his fancy car and rendered looks of suspicion. I smiled as usual but I couldn't tell if they were excited to see me, or if they were wondering whose car I got out of.

I went into the locker room, got dressed and started warming up for the game. My cousin entered the gym and had at least six hard looking guys trailing behind him. He waved at me and I returned a nod so people wouldn't know we were together. Then one of my teammates asked if I knew those guys. I was flushed with embarrassment and quickly lied, "Hell no. They look dangerous!" My teammate said, "Yeah, and I hope they're cheering for us or we might have to lose this game." The funny thing about a lie is that it'll reveal itself when it's ready.

After the game I came back to the half empty gym and I saw my cousin and most of his crew waiting on me. Full of humiliation, I walked over to them and was met with enthusiastic congratulatory comments. There were dozens of faces giving me strange looks and peering at me in disbelief but that wasn't the problem. When I scanned the crowd my uncle's eyes met mine along with a staunch look of disappointment. Without a word, he turned around and left. I expected an intense lecture from him when I arrived home.

I caught a ride with my cousin after the game and he casually slipped in that he needed to make a stop. He pulled alongside the curb in front of a store and told me to wait in the car. I was still excited about winning such a big game and began thinking about the direction of my life. Without warning, it happened again! While I was sitting in the car with one of my cousin's friends, my cousin came strolling out the store with a guy in a serious headlock position. My cousin's friend jumped out of the car and balled up his fist. They beat this guy up like he was a rag doll in a pitbull's mouth. Afterwards, my cousin dug into the guy's pockets and took his money while he laid in a fetal position on the ground groaning in pain. When I looked closer I recognized him, it was the guy who robbed me a while back. Now, I was the one who was shocked! My cousin's boldness in beating this guy didn't make sense because in my neighborhood, self-perseverance was a part of street life but revenge was the number one reason people were killed. I hung out with them for about an hour longer and they carried on like nothing ever happened. I'd seen enough to know I wasn't where I needed to be and decided to step away from jeopardizing my life and that of my son's.

LIFE: As a child we seem to glorify whatever we see the most of in our neighborhoods and homes. It doesn't matter what it is, a child's mind is going to gravitate towards what they deem as fun. Parents should ask, "What do you want to be in life?" This will provide them with a sense of direction and ability to establish goals to help your child stay on track. Have them write it down and then you teach them how to go about accomplishing their goals. Be strategic in your planning. For example, if your child wants to become a musician you should ask them what type of music or instrument they have interest in. Then, give them the information needed to make their goals become a reality. A musician will need to know how to read and write first. That is what school is for so it all goes hand in hand. The next phase is to explain the reality of what it will take to succeed such as, sacrificing hanging out all the time, spending money on wants instead of needs. Teach them to have stamina and never stop believing that they can make it! Show them positive stories instead of those that everyone tries to glorify like going to jail and then changing their life around. Sometimes that happens but it's not the change a lot of people need or make it out of. Then show them what it takes to be a successful musician as opposed to someone just wasting time, talking about what they want to do. Have them make a list of things they want to try and teach them how to earn the money to go out and get what they need. This will prevent them from taking the easy way out, which could be dangerous. The process is simple but the journey is the tough part. Prepare your children for the realities of life and they will be able to accept their own realities of being what they truly want to become.

When he dropped me off he told me to call him the next day but I made up a quick excuse and told him I was going to visit my half-sisters and brother who lived in another inner city housing complex, called Parkhill. He acknowledged and advised me to be careful because Parkhill was a tough neighborhood. He would know, so I conceded and went into my uncle's house ready for the storm. As soon as I opened the door I found my uncle resting placidly on the sofa. I anticipated his lengthy lecture but all he said was, "Great game." Without saying anything further he got up and headed for his bedroom. I walked into the kitchen and found a box of pizza on the table. I grabbed a few slices and returned to the living area where I slept. I let out a sigh of relief, kicked off my shoes and ultimately fell asleep with my clothes still on.

Early the next morning my uncle instructed me to get up and follow him outside. In the yard there was a lawn mower, pair of gloves, and a black trash bag. He instructed me to cut the grass, bag the leaves on the ground, and when I was done to wash the dishes, and mop the floors. He walked back inside leaving me to wonder what *he* was going through until he returned and began working alongside of me. Afterwards, we sat down in the kitchen and he explained that if I really wanted a better life I was going to have to work for it. I made him aware that I wasn't afraid of work but he gave clarity and said I'd have to work in the real world and not in the streets. I really didn't understand what he was talking about until he got upset and told me he found the twenty-dollar bill in my shoe. I'd forgotten to take it out and when I kicked my shoes off the money must have fallen out. He told me if I was going to do anything illegal or wrong in his house that I'd be putting him and his new wife in jeopardy. Trying to explain to him that I wasn't doing anything wrong was like talking to myself. Being a teenager and not knowing how to handle reality when confronted with it is a hard thing to except. Having lived in a shelter home a few years ago, now paying child support, and not having a steady job was a wakeup call that I had to keep fighting to fix. To pacify him and end the conversation, I said, "Yes sir." He said that would be our last conversation about it and I agreed, again.

The next day I walked a few miles to visit my two sisters and brother from my father's first marriage. They were pretty cool but I usually only hung around the younger sister because she worked at a community center and let me play basketball all the time. My older brother was much like my father. He had a quick temper and was known to fight a lot. My older sister was a hard worker and seemed to make her family a priority. I didn't get to see her often unless her boyfriend had a picnic during the summer and we'd hang out.

On a random afternoon I was walking to the store with my younger sister and we ran into my father's old friend Kane. My sister and I never liked him and he knew it but approached us anyway and asked my sister for money. Her attitude immediately changed and she cursed at him until he walked away. It was obvious he was on drugs. From what I was told he'd been living in the streets at that time. We walked back to the apartment and when I was leaving she handed me some money and my brother saw her. He got upset and told her she'd better not be doing anything illegal or he was going to tell our father. They began arguing but my older sister came in and broke them up. My sister and I slipped back outside as my older sister and brother started arguing. She told me that she was planning to move and that I could come stay with her if I wanted. I jumped at the opportunity and said, *yes*.

It was getting late so I headed back to my uncle's house. When I walked in, he handed me the newspaper. I took a deep breath and sat down, expecting to read something bad. It was a newspaper article describing the details of how well I played in the game the previous night. It was encouraging to see the newspaper cover an article that spoke of something I was doing well. The article mentioned how favorable my future looked as a star basketball player at my high school. My uncle smiled, then got up and walked away. I could tell he was proud of me and that made me feel proud, too.

I woke up and started cleaning the house. Then I grabbed my clothes and walked up the street to a Laundromat. I was truly happy, which was unusual for me. I stayed away from my cousin for a long time but eventually went looking for my sister to see if she moved into her new place, but I couldn't find her. We had become close, but then she moved without telling me, and I didn't see her for a while. I told my uncle I got a job at a store, which wasn't true. I still needed help and couldn't get it the way I wanted it from my uncle so I went back to my old neighborhood and reached out to my cousin again. He wasn't hard to find because he seemed to rise with the sun. He and his friends were excited to see me. My cousin called me, "Superstar," although I dismissed it as a joke. Then some of his friends that hadn't spoken to me before shook my hand and congratulated me. One of them asked for an autograph. My cousin pushed everyone away and told me to hop in the car and take a ride with him. All I really wanted to do was get some money and go spend time with my son, but it felt good to be recognized for something positive instead of being laughed at for looking like an abandoned child.

He drove for a long time while being very short with me and stayed on his cell phone the rest of the time. I thought to myself, he's about to go do something stupid while I'm with him again. He stopped at a corner liquor store where there were a lot of older men gathered outside. He told me to get out of the car and follow him. As we walked inside I could hear some of the guys whispering to one other. We walked up to the cashier and my cousin asked where my father was. I shook my head because I felt disrespected that he'd taken me there, but I was curious to hear the cashier's response. He simply stated that my father hadn't been by for a few days. The thought of us soliciting the whereabouts of my father caused my anger to heat up. I was furious when I left the store. There was an older guy leaning against the building as I exited and he mumbled enthusiastically, "He looks exactly like his father." I ignored him, went to the car, and waited for my cousin to come out. When he returned I let him have it! I asked why he'd do such a thing and he insisted that he felt I should be the one to break the silence between my father and I. I told him that there was no silence! He didn't give a damn about me and left, so that's all I needed to know. My cousin tried to make sense of things but I was too upset to listen to his rationalization at the time. My response to him was partially said out of anger but mainly spoken out of truth. With an intensifying tone of irritation I added, "If my father ever wanted to reach me he could've done what you did ... and found me."

That was the end of the conversation. I made my point and it didn't matter if he understood or not. His perspective wasn't my reality and I didn't feel that I needed anyone to repair a relationship that didn't exist. We jumped in the car and he drove me home. Hearing someone say that I looked like my father struck a nerve because deep down inside I really wanted to see him. The first time I thought about visiting him was out of sheer curiosity, but at this juncture it turned into a feeling of remorse. What if something happened to him and I never saw him again? What if he was actually a pretty decent guy? Once again the pain in my past kept me from trying to build a relationship with my father, especially since he didn't seem to want one either. The reality of the situation was that I wasn't able to forgive him.

LIFE: I've learned to forgive but only after learning how to love myself. If you love yourself don't hold onto destructive emotions such as anger, hatred, or resentment. This negativity will impede your personal growth and add additional physical and emotional stress that can be life threatening.

The pain in my past was temporary, but I was the one who made it last. I was consumed with what people thought about me instead of how I felt about myself. At that time, I wouldn't have accepted my father's forgiveness even if I were willing to see him because the anger from my childhood was flowing through my veins, contaminating my heart and mind.

I couldn't comprehend the problems my uncle George had with my choice to hang out with my cousin. I didn't know it at the time but my perspective was extremely narrow because I hadn't considered that hanging with the wrong crowd made me guilty by association. It took a while for me to learn this because no one was able to help me understand that logic until I was wrongfully accused of something that I was never a part of.

It was difficult to release my revolving hurt and anger after the positive contributions I've tried to make. In an instant, one individual's lie to try and save himself was intentionally aimed to destroy my name in the process. I was accused of having participated in violent activities. The media announced the information as if it were factual yet; neither the police nor anyone else had ever approached me to ask about the alleged incident. It was a manufactured lie that took forever before I received an apology. I didn't do anything illegal or violent but when you're the one everyone's eyes are on, at times, they may become jealous and decide to wreak havoc on your peaceful life in an effort to mirror their misery or create a name for themselves. Whatever the reason, you may never know.

I grew up in the inner city and that's where most of my friends lived, so when I hung around them, people associated me with the actions of my peers. It was either pick your career or your friendship. In the beginning, I chose my friendship but after realizing some of my friends weren't genuine, I decided to return loyalty to those who meant well. I won't abandon my friends because they've never judged me when I struggled as a child and I will never judge them now. I've made a conscious effort to do things I deem as productive and respectful for my family and my name. Additionally, I've given into the power of forgiveness and let go of negative emotions. Forgiving the people that hurt me the most was my way of releasing their power over me. My inability to forgive them was only keeping me from progressing in a healthy way. Anger and bitterness are destructive characteristics that no one should carry.

* * *

Chapter 11

WHEN WE FALL WE HAVE TO GET UP ON OUR OWN FIRST

My basketball career began to flourish and I continued to practice diligently. My uncle agreed to help pay child support so I could focus on my grades and that alone lifted a tremendous burden. Soon after, my ex-girlfriend moved without telling me and I wasn't able to see me son at all. Out of desperation, I started to find my way in life by following my uncle's leadership. It wasn't my plan, but the process my uncle established for me was working. I'd forgotten about some of the poor decisions I'd made and the occasions I disregarded my uncle's advice. The thought of those past decisions returning any repercussions had completely escaped me, yet some would return to collect with vengeance.

Nightfall was upon us when my friend Leon and I headed home from another friend's house. We noticed a few guys standing under a streetlight staring our way. We didn't pay them any attention and kept walking until one of the guys threw a bottle at us. We turned around and before we knew it they were already walking towards us. One guy yelled out, "You were the one who got me beat up!" As they came closer, I recognized him as being one of the guys who robbed me when I left the candy truck and the one that my cousin had beaten up in front of the store. But since I didn't let it go or try to stop my cousin, *I* had to deal with the consequences. With a burst of revenge he rushed towards me and his two friends rushed Leon. We start to fight but I quickly pinned him down. Without warning, I felt a sharp stick below my left shoulder. I jumped off of him and the guy was standing there with a brown paper bag. I couldn't make out what he had in the bag but we stood facing one another in silence. The guy looked like he was deliberating. Leon broke free from his fight and turned to grab my arm, pulling me away. We took off running as fast as our legs could move!

We erupted in laughter as we got closer to Leon's house but I had a terrible burning sensation in my back. I felt it while we were running but now my adrenalin was wearing off and the pain intensified. I reached for my back and pulled my shirt up but it was sticking to my skin and my movement caused the pain to increase. I pulled my shirt off and my friend looked like he was going into shock to see how much blood I'd lost. I thought I'd be okay until I saw the cut in the mirror. That guy had stabbed me!

Leon insisted that I go straight to hospital but I explained I couldn't even afford to take a basketball physical so I knew I couldn't get help with a stab wound. I asked him for some water and he told me to use peroxide so it wouldn't get infected. I conceded because I knew alcohol wound burn too much. He ran into the bathroom and grabbed a brown bottle, opened it and poured the peroxide on the puncture. That felt worse than when I was stabbed! I screamed so loud that his mother came running into his room and told us to be quite. Leon's facial expression was concerning and he was certain I'd have a serious problem if I didn't seek medical attention and have it stitched up. Regardless, we bandaged the wound and I went home without going to the hospital.

I arrived at my uncle's house, quickly acknowledged him, went straight into the bathroom and took off my shirt. I put on another one before he saw the blood. I was afraid to go to sleep because I was paranoid I'd bleed to death. I checked my back for the next two hours. It kept bleeding so I tried to stop it with a towel and cleaned the wound with peroxide. I feared the thought of being abandoned more than I feared death so I didn't tell my uncle; nonetheless it was a stupid decision to hide my injury. I understood that my choices literally affected my life.

The next morning I told my uncle I was going to stay with my mother but went to my friend Terrance's house instead. I was trying to hide my stab wound from my uncle but I didn't want him to know where I was going to be. He didn't like me venturing into my old neighborhood but that's where my friends were.

I was in my neighborhood and ran into my cousin whom I hadn't seen in a while. Before I headed back to my uncle's house, he gave me money to make sure I was okay. When I walked in, my uncle was waiting on me with a grave look. He sat me down and told me that he was tired of my lies and disrespect so I had to go live with my mother. I asked why and he said he saw my mother's friend and she told him that my mother had been in the hospital for two weeks. I couldn't believe this! I was doing so well but my lies caught up to me! He walked inside the house and all I could do was sulk in sorrow over my actions. While I was in the room packing I came to the realization that every one of my actions would have some kind of result. My heart wasn't hurting from my bad choices but from how I disappointed the one person who truly believed in me. I didn't want to lose the ground I was gaining and return to what I was trying to escape so I called my high school coach and asked Mr. Sayler if I could stay with him for a little while and he said, yes.

The next morning, I sat on the porch waiting on Coach Sayler. My uncle came out and sat next to me. I felt bad. Words couldn't express my disappointment or the pain I felt. I never made eye contact with him while he explained that I couldn't disrespect people who were trying to help me and that no one would tolerate my behavior. In a dismal tone all I said was, "Yes sir." When coach pulled up, I got up and walked away trying with great difficulty to keep my head up. I was tired of feeling like a throw away kid and I couldn't fathom how my uncle could be so dismissive. From his perspective, I wasn't putting in enough effort to get it right, but he was wrong. I was trying, but considering the deficit that I began with, I had a lot to learn and trusting my uncle was one of those things. The fact that I kept defying him was because I didn't have a constant authoritative figure in my life and he was only part-time because I chose to make it that way.

My uncle's resolution was showing me that I needed to grow-up and mature before that option was stripped from me. It was a harsh lesson to learn.

LIFE: In every child's life there will be learning curves in certain areas in which they will need guidance. As parents, once we learn where those curves are it's up to us to help straighten them out. Many parents consciously sweep their children's problems or areas of deficiency under the rug. When it's time for them to take responsibility for their actions they have difficulties understanding how to deal with life's consequences. To this day, I am remorseful for the disrespect and disappoint that I caused my uncle George. It took quite some time before I was able to display the reverence that he deserved. He didn't want anything from me other than what was best for me. My uncle willingly took on the job my parents had abandoned.

Upon entering my coach's tidy neighborhood it was apparent that we had very little in common. He was a thirty-year-old Caucasian and I was a fifteen-year-old African American teenage father. Our conversations about life helped me to learn a lot from him in a short period of time. Coach Sayler never appeared to judge me for anything, including my dysfunctional family or personal life.

While living with my coach, I didn't have the opportunity to see my friends or family as often because he lived a great distance away. Typically, after practice or following a game we'd return to his home, have dinner and watch television. Everything was progressing well until one particular day; I felt an uncomfortable tension in my body and knew something wasn't right. I was missing easy layups, falling to the ground a lot, and even missing free throws, which was rare. When I staggered to the bench to grab a drink of water, I spilled half of it down my mouth like I didn't have control over my body. We won the game, yet I didn't play particularly well. I returned to the locker room and slowly put on my sweats. I pulled open the door and entered the hallway to find my disgruntled cousin looking for me. I could tell by the look on his face that something was seriously wrong. When I reached him, he pulled me aside, looked directly into my eyes and completely devastated me. He told me that my baby sister was murdered while her daughter was inside the apartment. My rage had been dormant but quickly erupted like a volcano. As he sped over to the crime scene, he warned me that everyone knew who did it. I was rendered speechless when he said it was Kane, my father's best friend that killed her! I lunged into an emotional outburst while becoming reminiscent of the day Kane held me back while my father beat my mother for shooting him in the arm.

Since he was still at large, my cousin asked if I wanted to find Kane, but I realized that whenever I allowed my anger to respond it caused further damage. My niece was motherless and if I retaliated for her death, who would be there for my son?

That anger took a great deal of time before it waned and the sadness rested heavily inside of me for a long time. Besides my best friend Terrance, for many years I didn't get close to anyone, to avoid risking another loss.

While standing outside the funeral home of my sister's wake, I spotted my uncle George strolling towards me. He came to tell me something that he thought would raise my spirit. He said, my mother called and told him she just had a baby. I was thoroughly confused but he continued to elaborate. I struggled to register what he was saying. He stated that I had a little sister now and recommended that I go see her. I couldn't get a break from this madness! Instinctively, I bombarded him with questions. My incensed tone rang out in his ear and targeted reality in his head for a change. "Why did she have another child when she didn't take care of my brother and I? What's going to happen to my sister when my mother decides to live her *own* life again and doesn't come home for days to check on her? How will my sister feel when she has to sleep in a damn hallway while people just walk over her like she's invisible?" This time the dazed look was filtering across my uncle's eyes because he wasn't aware of anything I said. I continually protected my mother although the signs of neglect were prevalent for anyone that cared to see them, but they weren't for those who didn't. I wasn't able to handle the pain from losing my sister. I shook my head in disbelief that I was had a sister as though it were something to celebrate when we were about to bury another. I felt sorry for the baby and I was grieving for my sister. I blatantly walked away from my uncle without saying goodbye. After taking a single step, the conversation pushed me over the invisible precipice.

I thought I was beginning to take ownership of my life and carefully shape it into what I desired. Unfortunately, the problems were like a revolving door; while some went out others came in. As soon as things improved or stabilized, something agonizing would happen to throw me back in the cycle I was trying desperately to escape. I was always a step away from being in trouble, homeless, or dead and it hit the mark where it was taking its toll on me. The innate passion I had for basketball began to diminish while my passion for life went adrift. I wouldn't see my son for weeks at a time, call my cousin, or hang out with friends. I went to practice and back to my coach's home where I'd sit the duration of the day. He sensed something was wrong and continued to ask if everything was okay, but I'd say, *yes*, even when I didn't feel well. Habitually, my room became the hiding place I used to conceal my pain and the place that I'd lay and suffered through the horrible nightmares. It wasn't until a hefty jolt would thrust me from the dream and I'd find myself drenched in cold sweat, alone.

It took some time to get used to the living arrangements but once Coach Sayler started helping me open up, I trusted I had someone in my corner who truly cared for my well-being. We engaged in conversations about what I *used to like* about basketball, my favorite food, or if I knew how to cook. I told him I could cook and asked if he had any bologna and bread. I told him I could cook the best, fried bologna sandwich he ever had. He laughed and replied, "I don't eat bologna." I was shocked! I'd never met someone that didn't eat fried bologna. The variances between our cultures didn't affect the way he treated me and we actually laughed about my specialty in frying bologna. Coach and I made a bet that if I got more than two turnovers per game that I had to cook his favorite meal. I agreed and he proceeded to teach me how to cook pasta dishes and prepare salads. I had the time of my life learning how to cook but I enjoyed the bond he and I created during that time even more. After we had a few more straightforward discussions about life, we gained a mutual respect beyond sports that transcended into a friendship.

The passion that was driving me into a better realm returned. I finished out my junior year as a top player in the city and received offers from several Division I colleges. I asked my coach to advise me on the school I should select however; he told me it was solely my decision. Being able to choose my own college was the first sign that I could make major decisions on behalf of my future without it being a choice between where to sleep or how to find money to buy food.

The summer leading into my senior year was great. Since the first time I picked up a basketball, I dreamt of going to the University of Louisville or Kentucky. I remember practicing each player's moves until I had mastered it in my mind. I played defense like Billy Thompson from the University of Louisville but acted as if I were Kenny "Sky" Walker from the University of Kentucky, and dunked over him. I learned to dunk off one leg and soar like one of the Kentucky players, Rex Chapman, while making clutch free throws like a Louisville player, Milt Wagner. I added my own twist to try and make them better moves so I could be better than those guys if I ever played them. That opportunity actually came to fruition one day when I rode with my friend Jason Osborne and his uncle David to the University of Louisville campus and played a pick-up game with my cousin James "Boo" Brewer. Boo always picked me before some of his teammates and while they were trying to figure out why, he was teaching me to play with effort so my talent would show during the games. The games were incredible. I'd guard the former Kentucky Mr. Basketball, Dwayne Morton or another great player named Everick Sullivan. The games were intense and I wanted to be better than them so I made it a point not be star-struck but to become an equal, in their eyes. I valued playing against them and it actually made me a much better player affording me the opportunity of being challenged by playing against superior players. Boo would always advise me on playing defense and guide me through the plays if I messed up. It was like having a teammate and a coach at the same time. I took the knowledge and went back to play in the summer league games at my high school.

I played against some of the other top high school players and after beating everyone with little effort I ended up playing against a guy named Jayson. Jayson was left-handed and had a pretty good game but I was confident that he couldn't beat me so when we played I was horsing around with him. After he was ahead of me by a couple of baskets, I decided to take him seriously, but it was too late! I tried everything in my power to stop him but he was hitting every shot he aimed at the basket. I made an impressive comeback but I missed the game-winning shot. I checked the ball up and I remember Boo telling me to guard a player's strong hand and take away his best moves. I did just that but he drove with his right hand and made an incredible layup, right in my face. I was so angry because I hadn't lost a one-on-one game before and he actually beat me. After the game Coach Sayler came up to me and insisted, "You're a better player than him but he played harder than you from start to finish." I realized that my confidence quickly turned into arrogance and unfortunately, that arrogance rolled into disappointment. I couldn't blame anyone but myself and after that game I was determined not to ever lose another one-on-one game again, and I didn't.

That same day I arrived home from our high school summer league. Coach had two voicemails on the answering machine. One was from Western Kentucky's assistant coach, Tom Crean, and the other was from the head coach of the Kentucky Wildcats, Rick Pitino. I wasn't familiar with Western Kentucky because the only two colleges I wanted to play for were at the University of Louisville or the University of Kentucky. Those were the only two teams that everyone in the inner city ever cheered for. I used to think if I made it to either one of those schools I'd be respected in the neighborhood as someone who worked hard to make it out. I received several letters from schools but I wouldn't open them because I was waiting on a letter from either, Louisville or Kentucky.

After Coach Rick Pitino of the University of Kentucky called and said he wouldn't have any more scholarships available until the following year, my coach and I focused on Louisville. It seemed like it took forever to receive a letter to visit the University of Louisville except by then, I was only marginally enthusiastic because in the interim, I considered other options, and my first choice was Syracuse University.

The 1992 season started off great and I continued to play extremely well. I acquired a lot of attention emanating citywide, while my coach received a consistent call volume from college coaches making inquiries. Letters from colleges poured in, increasing my confidence. *I was happy* and it pushed me to study more and practice even harder. I was beginning to understand how my sacrifices became beneficial and overshadowed the negativity my life had been laden with.

My life was flowing in the right direction. I was happy to see my best friend excelling in football and I was the top player in the region and state. Our first game was against a tough team but I had grown another two inches, was now 6'6 and had far more confidence combined with less stress. After a game one evening, I went to Leon's house; he lived directly behind my uncle George. I didn't know what caused it but I wanted to see my uncle. I barely knocked on the door before he answered. Uncle George was as happy to see me, as I was to see him. In fact, he acted as if nothing ever transpired between us. I apologized for my disrespectful actions towards him and the immature decisions I made. He accepted my apology and hugged me. I realized how much I had grown from a child into a young man. I told my coach that I wanted to move back with my uncle and he supported my decision acknowledging first that he'd always be there, if I ever needed him. I was fortunate to have two men that made substantial sacrifices in their own lives to help me. There is truth in the saying, "It takes a man to raise a man." The discipline that a man with positive and sincere intentions can provide a young adult is the difference between that young man surviving or dying mentally or physically at the hands of his own decisions. Learning how to control your emotions to progress instead of regress is the key.

Upon transitioning back to my uncle George's house we sat and engaged in lengthy dialogue about rules and life. He told me that a man is only a man when he admits his mistakes, forgives himself as he forgives others, and works hard to provide for his family. I was being taught something that I had never been told before and it was something that I wanted all young men to understand. I put on my mature mask and went to find my son. I hadn't seen my son in a long time and when I found him I saw how fast he had grown-up but it was without me. I made the conscious effort to spend every weekend I could with him. Although he didn't know it, my son helped mold me into the man I am today.

I started to do things with Derek Jr. instead of with my friends. I relinquished the time I spent with my best friend to increase the time with my son. I felt the difference it made to my son when *I* made him smile as opposed to never having a hand in helping create and then experience the joy behind it. I was careful to follow my uncle's instructions and I started to see the difference it made in my life. I continued to do well on the basketball court and take care of my son. I was able to earn my uncle's trust again and we became like father and son. My life was working.

Change in life is inevitable and it made no exception in mine. When you have the plight and inconsistencies that I experienced it can become discouraging, debilitating, and frustrating, which has the tendency to break you along with your faith.

When I arrived in the gymnasium I noticed the University of Louisville's coach, seated in the stands. I put my game mask on to hide my emotions and went to work having a great game along the way. It was filled with notable dunks and highlighted plays. We won by a large margin. The Louisville coach left without speaking a word but I felt pretty good about my performance. Later in the season he returned to watch another game and again, I played well. We beat our cross-town rivals, the Fairdale Bulldogs in their own gym.

It was brought to my attention that the two top players in the state were considering the University of Louisville, as well. It was time for the King of the Bluegrass tournament, in Kentucky and we played against a top player named Tick Rogers. He was my height and could really play. Since we were the top two recruits in the state the crowd was in anticipation of us playing hard against one another. Tick's team was a bit shorter than mine, and when I realized their point guard was only 5'10, I was prepared to take complete advantage of the matchup. It was the first play and I looked at my teammate, Stephon Sheckles switched and popped outside to let me go down to the post area. He popped out and then threw the ball to our best passer on the team, Shawn Fugitt, and he threw a back door alley-op to me! I turned and dunked on my opponent with a 43-inch vertical leap that was just hard! I felt bad and rubbed his head jokingly even causing him to laugh. We destroyed them by 25 points by the time it was over. My teammate Chris Travis guarded Tick most of the game and made Tick work for every point he made. It was clear that I had a better showing in that game but Tick was still an incredible player.

The opportunity to play against Dequan Wheat who was in a different region, never happened but he was an amazing player. I told my uncle that I would love to play with those guys one day causing him to question if I had received an offer from the University of Louisville. He informed me that Dequan and Tick had already received one. I thought about it because my uncle and I had many discussions about where I should attend college. He wanted me to go to North Carolina or Kentucky because they seemed to be a better fit for my personal style. Furthermore, he wanted me to get out of the city and expand my mind. I didn't understand why he felt that way until I actually went to Las Vegas and played in a Christmas tournament. The bright flashing lights were more colorful than anything I'd ever seen, especially given the darkness that seemed to blanket my neighborhood.

We played against some truly great players such as, Dion Cross from Arkansas, and Derek Fisher who went on to play in the NBA for the Los Angeles Lakers. I learned what it meant to maintain my focus and to be a leader. I had three great games and led my team to the championship game where I hit two free throws with no time left on the clock. It was that particular tournament that helped develop me into a stronger leader because everything I did with passion, discipline and focus caused my teammates to follow ... they believed in me.

When we returned home I continued to play well and the assistant coach at Ohio State, attended a tournament game in Kentucky. I broke all kinds of records that day. I had a triple double, 39 points, 18 rebounds, and 14 assists. He spoke to my coach and said he and the head coach would love for me to visit their campus, so I did. Columbus was a beautiful city and I loved it because my uncle's wife had family there and they were great people. I decided that I couldn't wait on Louisville to offer me a scholarship so I started looking at schools other than Syracuse. I made visits to Western Kentucky, South Carolina, and The Ohio State University. The funny thing was that out of the three, Western Kentucky was my favorite because of their assistant coach Tom Crean. When I was close to making a decision, the University of Louisville's assistant coach, called. They wanted me to visit but my excitement had dissipated. Nevertheless, I went to see the Louisville coach at his home. Dequan Wheat was on his visit at the same time. As it turned out, I had a blast. He was a pretty good guy and we spoke for a long time. We even imagined playing in the backcourt together executing incredible plays to win a championship for our hometown. That situation sounded great but along came life.

* * *

Chapter 12

Signing Day Surprise

It was 1992 and the last six years of my life felt like sixty years of frustration, anger and constant education whether or not I wanted it. Time continued to evolve and so did my reality. Basketball was my safe haven. It was what I knew best, revered the most, and learned to trust. The game forced me to make choices that protected the authenticity of my character. It helped me find myself, provided light in my dark world and when it was dark it helped me to master my foul shots. Basketball helped me envelop the impact of positive thinking and it imparted the ability to have genuine respect for the game, others, and myself.

I had a great season as did Tick and Dequan. Dequan and I had stayed in contact since our visit. He hadn't passed his test yet and I hadn't signed. Both of us were on the fence in regards to our status for the next year. In the meantime, Tick had already agreed to sign with Louisville. My uncle advised me on topics that I needed to discuss with Louisville's head coach. Instead of allowing a team to randomly pick me I needed to ensure that we were a good fit for one another. Uncle George wanted me to find out where he saw me fitting in and if he would redshirt me since there were so many of the same players coming back. I assured my uncle that I'd outwork them so it didn't bother me. He said he believed me but advised me to make sure I knew exactly what I was getting before I made my decision. Time passed without any calls so I reached out to their assistant coach and said I wanted their head coach to meet with my uncle to discuss my future on their team. He said okay and that he'd get back to me. The first week went by and no word. I called the following week and left a voice mail with no response. Then I received a call from Dequan congratulating me on winning "Mr. Basketball" because the news reported I was the favorite since we finished the regular season as the number one team in the state and my all around numbers were better than everyone else's. I told Dequan that *he* was the favorite because they made it to the state tournament and he should win it. We both woke up the next morning to learn that Tick Rogers had won Kentucky's "Mr. Basketball" and I was surprised to say the least. I was disappointed that I didn't win but I was more upset that I couldn't manage a callback from Louisville's coaches. Since I hadn't heard from Louisville, I scratched them off my list. That same day, the Ohio State coach called and asked if I'd rendered a decision yet. I said *no* because we hadn't taken time to discuss my future plans. He said he'd be in front of me by the end of the day. I was impressed. His effort displayed their desire for me to be a part of their team. He and his assistant drove four hours in a rental car from Columbus, Ohio to Louisville, Kentucky that same day. He told me that no matter what; I'd play because I was smart enough to figure things out. I gave him my word that he would be the first person I called after I received the results of my ACT.

Several days later, I finally received a call from the assistant coach at Louisville. He said my uncle and I should visit the campus and talk to the head coach when he had time. We only lived ten minutes away from the university's campus and he wouldn't make time to speak with my uncle but another coach willingly drove four hours to speak to me the same day. I took Louisville off my radar and as soon as I received my test scores I didn't hesitate to call Ohio State to say that I was going to play there!

It was disconcerting that I wasn't able to play for one of my home teams and the lack of professionalism in which I was handled. Louisville's disinterest in making time to properly discuss questions we had about their program encouraged me to remind him. If we ever played against one another I would be sure to show them that they made a poor decision.

People stated that I made a bad decision in leaving the state. My friends cautioned me to stay home but what they didn't know was that, I wanted to stay home but the opportunity had not presented itself. With misguided information, people questioned my decision and doubted me as if they really wanted me to fail. I realized a lot of those people didn't know my struggles and had no idea that I wouldn't stop until I found a way! I had constructed my own way of thinking because I was ready to live the way I wanted to without struggling or living with regrets. People I alleged were friends continued to talk behind my back, predict I'd never make it, and contend I'd be home in less than a year. Those words merely added fuel to my already burning passion of never giving in or up!

LIFE: A fake friend is worse than having a thousand enemies! They are privy to many of our emotions, personal thoughts, and true character. When the fallout comes, they become the first person to exploit your vulnerabilities when they don't get what they want. Be very vigilant as to whom you call your friends because I have been a friend to people who only wanted to use my name or status to elevate themselves and once they felt I wasn't on top anymore or had nothing to offer, they showed their true character and turned into people I never knew. We all go through it because the same unexpected manner in which you meet friends is the same way you will lose them, unexpectedly.

* * *

Chapter 13

YOUR JUDGEMENT IS YOUR OWN

Everything was going well and I was excited to have an opportunity to live in the proximity of peace. The amusing aspect of my life was that I had spent so much of it dealing with problems that almost intuitively I could sense trouble heading my way. A week prior to my leaving for college, I made a decision that went against my instincts.

A close friend of mine, Herb from Doss High School invited me to a college party. Herb attended the University of Louisville on a football scholarship, and became a star player after his first year. I thought about going because it was on campus and I wanted to experience what it would have been like to visit that campus. For some reason, I decided to stay home for the balance of the day. Then that one tragic night, the phone rang and it was a call from my friend Tracy. He sounded hysterical, and after his words finally made it past his crying, he announced, "Herb was just shot!" I jumped out of bed with my head painfully ready to explode.

When Tracy hung up the phone, guilt raced through my body. I felt guilty for not being there like he had been for me just a few years earlier. Herb's parents always welcomed people into their home and not once did they turn down any of the kids in the neighborhood, including me. When I stayed over, Herb treated me like I was his own brother and would give up his bed so I could sleep comfortably for a change.

All night long I struggled to grasp what had transpired. I even wondered if I'd gone to the party would I have been shot instead of him? I was in complete dismay because again, it seemed that my life was full of so many signs and directions, that I didn't know which one to follow.

The next day I went to visit my friend in the hospital and although he looked normal Herb wasn't able to move. I stayed there for hours while several people came by to check on him. By the time I returned home that evening, I received another call from Tracy. This time he told me that Herb was paralyzed.

That night I prayed for Herb to be strong and I asked God to please grant me the ability to live long enough to make it to college. I guess I couldn't see much further than that.

That was the point I decided that I would determine my own outcome. I started attending church with my uncle George and aunt Glenda. Although I didn't fully understand the Bible I was cognizant that I'd been pulled through inconceivable situations by the hand of God. As time passed and situations grew worse, I felt God constantly working in my life. When I felt I was alone, God picked me up, dusted me off, and gave me inspiration by way of another opportunity. Without fail, he sent people to help me when I was scared and alone. When I look back and see everything I overcame I acknowledge that I kept fighting because I knew there had to be something better. God was testing my strength, adjusting my focus, and planting my feet firmly in faith. God was my guide when I couldn't see His vision for me.

* * *

Chapter 14

GROWING UP ISN'T AN OPTION

My uncle George and his wife, Glenda drove me to The Ohio State University and I couldn't believe I made it that far. My aunt Glenda was a tremendous support and went to several of my games, In fact, most people thought she was my mother. I never knew if Glenda ever loved me as a son, but she showed me how much she cared and that was all I could've asked for. Glenda's family in Columbus became my extended family. Earnest and Brenda kindly welcomed me into their home and provided uplifting encouragement.

I experienced more positivity as I grew older but my uncle was the only person on my mother's side to receive a college degree. He reminded me of the significance an education would have on my future and drove that in more than anything else. He was my rock and the strong foundation that I leaned on. He helped shape me into the man I was becoming. He believed in me when I didn't believe in myself and refused to settle for anything less than me arriving where I was standing and taking it from that point. I needed my uncle George but didn't always know how much.

As soon as he dropped me off at my dorm room, I went the wrong way. My new roommate was much like my cousin. He was a lot of fun but had a temper that took an army to control. We became cool and hung out together until I saw him doing more partying than schoolwork. I slowed down my hanging out with him and started to hang with another dorm mate of mine who played football, Jason. We became best friends and hung out most of the time as if we were childhood friends. He was from Columbus so I'd visit his old high school and his home. We made plans to drive to my hometown so he could see my high school and hang out during the Kentucky Derby.

Jason rushed into my room one day and told me to hurry up and get dressed because some of his teammates were at a party. He insisted it would be fun. I was spending time with my new girlfriend so I couldn't go. He told me that he wouldn't go if I didn't, so I told him to give me an hour and Jason said he'd come back to get me.

I didn't think much of it until I received a call a few hours later. It was our other roommate telling me that Jason was in a car wreck. I went into panic mode and tried to find out what hospital he was in. I sat next to the phone impatiently waiting to hear back. It seemed like it took forever before our dorm mate called. He told me that Jason died.

I threw the phone against the door and completely broke down in my room. I couldn't escape the pain. The entire time I was wondering, what if I had gone with him, could I have stopped him from driving?

I didn't feel guilty but I believed if I were with him I could have made a difference.

After Jason's funeral I kept to myself the majority of time. I embraced being alone because it allowed time for me to reflect on my choices and the direction of my life. The roommate I had at the time was a teammate and he decided to slow down as well. We focused more on basketball and became solid friends. During a preseason game, I broke my right hand, which caused me to miss the first game of my season. The setback was disappointing but there was nothing I could do other than work harder because no one in Columbus knew who I was and I needed to validate my aptitude.

Weeks later I was finally able to play in a tournament game in Portland, Oregon. That was the first game of my college career and I was given Player of the Game honors. I came back to Columbus and began to excel in basketball and gained the respect and attention from Buckeye fans. I was the Player of the Month several times in Ohio and was even nominated for All Big Ten honors. That was a tremendous honor because the league consisted of Jalen Rose, Chris Webber, Jimmy King, Ray Jackson, and Juwan Howard, better known as The Fab Five. In addition, it included the best college player I ever had the opportunity to see play, *in person*, Glen "Big Dog" Robinson, of the Purdue Boilermakers. Other star players were, Calbert Chaney and Damon Bailey of the Indiana Hoosiers, Shawn Respert and Eric Snow, of the Michigan State Spartans, Michael Finley of the Wisconsin Badgers, and Voshon Leonard of the

Minnesota Gophers. That league had a plethora of first round NBA draft choices and I was just happy to be mentioned in the same breath.

It was winter break of that same season and we stayed in a hotel across from our basketball gymnasium. I invited my new girlfriend to come by so we could hang out after practice. It was fun and harmless as we both were young and didn't have any worries. I started spending a lot of time with her and we grew very close. Her mother was supportive of our relationship and treated me well. I'd typically stay at her home until it got late and she'd do the same at my place. Although it was puppy love, I felt it forming into a close friendship that was meant to last.

My teammate and I had a great freshman season. We were the top two candidates for Freshman of the Year honors. Reminiscent of my senior year in high school, many people assumed I was going to win, but as it turned out I lost again. It was a tough loss. I began to taste the thrill of victory and didn't like losing at anything. I congratulated my teammate and went to practice, alone in the gymnasium. I was working out when the head coach walked in and saw me playing by myself. He asked why I was playing alone when I could have someone rebound for me. I explained that I preferred to work out alone.

I reverted back to playing in the same manner I had when I was alone in the neighborhood park venting about my situation at home. Practicing alone was a way for me to release my pain and anger. I stopped, and took a good look at the beautiful arena I was standing in and then released a broad smile. Only a few years prior I was sitting in a drug infested neighborhood without any thought of what my future would bring. In order to change the direction of my life I embraced focus, maintained a superior level of discipline, ramped-up my drive and lived with passion to arrive at this opportunity. I put the happy mask on and went back to my room and congratulated my teammate again, but this time properly. I started to understand that even though I lost the award, I already had more than I ever imagined. My gifts were coming by the way of happiness.

The summer arrived and I didn't have enough money to return to Kentucky so I decided to stay in Columbus. I played in a summer league for Mark Masser who loved basketball just as much as I did. He had a passion for helping those who helped themselves, and he made sure our summer league team had the best of everything. We went undefeated and won the summer league with ease. Our team consisted of Nick Van Excel, Corey Blount, Herb Jones, and other great college players. Mark Masser took me under his wing and taught me more than sports. He taught me the value of working hard for things and what to do when I achieved them. Mark reinforced what the true value of family was while his wife Sonny and their daughters Julie, Dana, and Jenny accepted me. They displayed more love than I received from my own family. I was astounded by the way they didn't judge me and humbled by their interest in me. They would ask if I were okay. I'm used to people looking out for themselves but when they called, it was to ask how *I* was doing.

After the summer league I was selected to play in the Junior Olympics in San Antonio, Texas. I met a lot of great players and some of them became close friends of mine. The league consisted of North Carolina signees, Jerry Stackhouse, Rasheed Wallace and Jeff McGinnis. My uncle loved that I had to play against them instead of with them. When I called my uncle he told me that if I couldn't join them, then I'd better beat them. I understood that if I wanted to win awards that I had to earn them without leaving any doubt that I was better than most.

The teams consisted of four regions, the East, West, North, and South. My team was the North and although we didn't have the top talent we knew how to win as a team. Our point guard Jacque Vaughn who was attending The University of Kansas, was one of the best players I had ever played with. Jacgue and I were in tune with one another from the first day of practice. We were able to read each other's thoughts perfectly. The games were pretty competitive but to me, it was like playing basketball in my old neighborhood and reliving the highlight moments of winning a championship. From the first game until the last, I focused on dominating everyone that played against me and it worked! Our team won the Gold medal and I was named the Most Valuable Player. Regardless of the plight I had in my childhood, I'd finally proven *I could achieve anything if I believed I could!*

Once school began, I had to travel a lot because the basketball season was in full swing. I was having a great season until things began to shift in the wrong direction. I met another girl that stayed in the same dorm building as I did. One day we were hanging out in my room. I left for a couple of minutes and when I returned she was deep in the middle of a conversation. I looked at her with curiosity until I noticed the sarcastic expression on her face when she handed me the phone. I took the phone and heard my girlfriend's disgruntled voice. She said that she was on her way to see me.

After I hung up the phone, I asked my new friend why she answered my phone. She shrugged her shoulders and asked why I didn't tell her I had a girlfriend. She said she didn't mind that I had a girlfriend but I should've told her the truth. I was surprised that she handled it with maturity and remained composed. She explained that it didn't bother her because she had a boyfriend that lived out of town and she just wanted to be with me because I was the star on campus. Her honesty made me feel somewhat important until I realized I was being used because of my position. We laughed about the situation and she agreed to call me later, after I spoke with my girlfriend. This was the first time I had anyone say they liked me for my status and it was my first understanding of how fame can cloud a person's mind and impair their judgment. When my girlfriend arrived I explained what transpired and apologized. However, we agreed to break-up and she left without an argument or any emotion at all.

That break-up caused me to be more direct and become more of a free spirit when it came to relationships. I didn't think about consequences after that. I told myself I would never cheat on any other girlfriend. My rational was if I didn't date her then I wasn't cheating. I casually returned to making excuses to meet different women the same way I did to find a place to sleep when I was a kid.

I was having the game of my life against the Michigan Wolverines. I was the leading scorer and coach allowed me to direct our team the way I saw fit in order to win the game. I was playing one-on-one against a great player named Jimmy King. I made a quick move and felt my left knee pop like a rubber band! That pain shot through my body causing me to scream so loudly that the entire crowd instantly grew silent. The Michigan players tried to help, as did my teammates but there was nothing anyone could do. They stood there, gathered around me as if I were about to die. They looked as though they knew something I didn't.

After being examined by a doctor he informed me that my season was over because I had torn all of the ligaments in my knee. I couldn't think and I didn't know how to respond. I was afraid because I was being stripped of the very thing I fought to have and I was devastated because all indications were that my career was over! Once again, I started thinking about the type of job I could get and I wondered if I could open a candy truck like the Whiteside family had done. I was slammed with reality and realized that the life I was living was a gift and no longer a game. I was ready to begin my tumultuous journey and figure it out. I didn't know what else to do but prepare to survive.

A few days passed and I was giving up on being optimistic about my surgery. I was tired of worrying and my positivity was turning into doubt. At the point I felt defeated God sent a few powerful messages that came when I needed to hear them most. I received two calls from NBA players Mark Price and Ron Harper. Mark told me to keep my head up and that my surgeon would do a great job. When Ron called he told me that he had the same surgery and if I worked really hard I would be able to play again and still have the same game. Their words were humbling. The encouragement they returned to me was uplifting and gave me the confidence to believe my career was still on the court, if I wanted it. In the darkness came yet another light when I thought my dream was ending.

Doing something for someone without any reason other than to encourage them can help change that person's life. Later that day, I received a call from my old coach, Terrance Moorman. He reminded me how hard I worked to get to that point and said I'd just have to work harder. He took time to say a powerful prayer and left that on my heart. I really didn't know how to respond because I'd only gone to church a few times with my uncle. I listened to him, remained open to receive the blessings, and went to have surgery.

When I was driven to the hospital I saw my face on a billboard. I was wheeled into the hospital in a wheelchair by an older man that didn't have any idea who I was. He told me that I have a purpose in life and I should accept that purpose from God. He wished me luck as I was wheeled into my room. The female nurse that checked my vitals for surgery said I had a great attitude regarding the surgery and that she'd pray for me. I began to get scared because everyone mentioned God the entire time as if my surgery was going to kill me. I thought I should open my mind and heart and pray to have the strength to endure my surgery. I thought God should hear from me, too.

After my surgery I woke up to Mark and Sonny Masser standing in the room smiling over me. My head coach walked in and I smiled even harder. What a great vision. I felt the impact of the medication after an unsuccessful attempt to sit upright. I glanced up and watched my uncle appear like an angel, and then drifted soundly back to sleep. I didn't know how long I was asleep but by the time I woke up again, everyone was gone. I didn't know if it was a dream or if I was standing alone in defeat again.

LIFE: Negative thoughts are toxic to your psyche and many times we choose to hold onto them. Shifting your focus to the positive aspects of your life or inspirational reflections will help you deliver what you want to acquire. You can't worry and pray at the same time as they contradict one another. Only one of them is effective while the other is damaging and can lead you to the negative emotion of hopelessness.

I started my rehab program with a woman named Lind. Lind did a phenomenal job helping people return to good health after an accident or injury. Lind's style of rehabilitating people was a smooth blend of motivation and a hefty dose of hard work. While I was beginning to believe that I felt much better and ready to take on more, my doctors told me that although the surgery was successful, it would still be at least another five months before I could play. That meant I would miss the beginning of my junior season and risk not having enough time for proper training and development. The news hit my core. I wasn't ready to hear that but since it was my reality, some of the toxins were beginning to seep back into my thoughts and circulate comfortably in my head. By the time I returned to my dorm room I had more discouraging news awaiting my arrival. As I approached my room I saw two campus police officers standing in the hallway. They questioned me about my roommate and his whereabouts but I told them I didn't have any idea where he'd be. They left without saying anything further. When I finally settled in my room, I turned on the television and couldn't believe what flashed on the screen. The local news said that two of my other teammates had allegedly stolen gas and were on the run. I was in disbelief over the luck we were having and unhappy with how quickly things were falling apart. After seeing the bad news I decided to rethink my future.

My cousin called to tell me his mother had cancer and was about to pass so I left Columbus as quickly as I could and took the Greyhound home. When I arrived, I found my cousin completely distraught. After spending time trying to help him deal with his situation, I went to see my son. His mother got into trouble, which placed him in a bad situation. It could have led to my son being in the same cycle that I inherited as a kid. My uncle George found a lawyer for me and we fought his aunt for custody of my son. She wanted to keep custody of him and his brother, which I didn't have a problem with as long as I was able to keep him during the summer. I thought about getting an apartment for just the two of us so I could focus on him. I didn't understand why she'd fight me for custody of my son until I heard her ask for a large amount of money. It was sickening that a person would care more about money then to allow a child to grow up with his own father. The ruling was passed and the judge didn't think I'd have enough time to raise my son and awarded split custody between the both of us. It was a cutting decision that the court system wouldn't allow me to have custody of my son but what was even more hurtful was the contemptuous effort from his aunt to keep my child from me. I accepted the terms because we couldn't afford to pay the lawyer any more money. It was my first taste of how the court system *doesn't* work but it wouldn't be my last.

* * *

Chapter 15

WHEN WINNING ISN'T ENOUGH

While I was making my visits in Louisville I ran into my old friend Kevin who was attending the University of Kentucky. He told me to come to a campus party and hang out with him for the weekend. I agreed because their classes commenced a month prior to mine. Later that night, I went to the party and had a great time. But when I walked around the campus, I fell in love with everything. The basketball players had solid characters and the students loved the team. I thought about the benefits if I lived an hour away from my son instead of four hours. I figured if I were to redshirt and sit out that year I could spend the time returning to a healthier physical state without losing a year of eligibility. It made sense but I really loved everything about Columbus and Ohio State. The final decision came when I received a call from my aunt and she told me that my great-grandmother had passed away. We lost the rock of our family. My uncle was the closest to her so he really took it hard. We had a long conversation over the phone. Deep in memories of her I mournfully listened to him expressing his hurt and how difficult it was to lose his best friend, my great-grandmother. I could easily distinguish the hurt in my uncle's heart. It was so prevailing that it pushed me to return home and try to help the little family I had left.

The day of my great-grandmother's funeral was the first time I'd seen my mother or brother in years. While my uncle and I were sitting in the funeral home, viewing my great-grandmother's body, we noticed my mother walking into the building with her male friend. I could tell she had been drinking, which caused my hurt and anger to reemerge. My expression gave a response to the lack of respect she displayed upon entering the church. I wanted to keep my sentiments to myself but I told my uncle George I didn't want to be there if my mother was. Besides, after all this time, I knew she was aware that neither of us really had anything to say to one another. My uncle attempted to do damage control prior to us conversing and asked me to be nice and respectful towards her for the sake of my great-grandmother.

My tainted emotions were already elevated from the passing of my great-grandmother. Trying to be respectful to someone that showed me tremendous disrespect, allowed me to struggle, and fend for myself as a child, was nearly impossible. Uncle George saw the frustration in my eyes and upon my face, but asked me to do it for him. I agreed, only because I loved my uncle as a father, and I still loved my mother, regardless of our past relationship.

My mother strolled into the funeral home at a mildly unsteady pace and casually approached me. She positioned herself in front of me and reached to give me a hug. After returning a light hug I caught her glaring at me with a confused expression, she said, "I hear you're in college and that you're doing good." In a derisive tone I replied, "I'm fine." Those two little words upset her. Allowing her anger to escape and flow out in a contemptuous tone she replied, "Don't get smart with me. I'm still your mother!" I shook my head in dismay and stated, "I love you, but a mother would *never* have left me like you did." I tried to walk away but she grabbed my arm and gripped it tightly. Her boyfriend tried to calm her down but I yanked away and headed out the door. My uncle came over and restrained my mother in an effort to help her grab hold of her composure instead of me. He was as transparent as I was when it came to my mother. I could tell he was disappointed but in an effort to neutralize the situation he walked her into the viewing room to pay her respect. I was infuriated with her while at the same time saddened that I couldn't give her a real hug. I sat in the hallway until my mother left the funeral home. When she did I got up and went to sit down next to my uncle. It was hard because deep inside, I wanted her in my life. She left the funeral home and we didn't see each other for several years ... again.

It was getting late and my brother was still a no-show. Ultimately, he ended up arriving but acted as if nothing was wrong with his lack of punctuality. We briefly shared a dry hello sounding as if we barely knew one another, and then he walked past me to view our great-grandmother. When he came out, I was still angry, which caused me to snap, "Why are you so damn late?" Although I tried to be peaceful I couldn't tolerate so much intentional disrespect. An inappropriate shouting match began until my uncle broke us up as my brother shouted, "I wish we weren't brothers and I hope I don't ever see your ass again!" Although I was a little stunned, his angry words settled in my soul in a familiar way that I was used to. I replied, "If you see me, don't ever speak!" Our hurtful words were somewhat anticipated especially after the way he left several years prior leaving too many bitter years of absence between us. Being home quickly pulled my unresolved anger out and it began to shape me. I had to find a way to deal with my past and return the focus to my future.

As I was headed back to Columbus I became sick because I had a lot to deal with and the hardest was telling my college coach, who believed in me, that I wanted to transfer. On top of that, I had the pain of telling the Masser family I was leaving after everything they'd done to help me become a better person. It was the most painful and difficult decision that I ever had to make.

* * *

Chapter 16

THE TRANSFER INTO
THE TRANSFORMATION

The time arrived and I made the painful but joyous decision to transfer to the University of Kentucky, to play for Coach Rick Pitino. The true excitement I had in transferring was that he was going to allow me to play exactly how I wanted to play. Lexington was only an hour away from Louisville and since I had to sit out one full season, I was able to build a stronger bond with my son. My uncle and I were also able to spend more time together. He'd drive down after work to watch me play. The move seemed to be exactly what I needed and it made my life so much easier since I was more focused and determined to be the best amongst the best.

The new season started as I was just finding my way on the team. I had reconnected with some old friends that played with me in the McDonalds Derby Festival game from high school. Tony Delk and Walter McCarty were great teammates and welcomed me in with no problem. I fit right in with our team. Our team had an effortless way of doing everything together as a group. We went to movies, dinner, laser tag, and bowling, as much as possible. This was extremely abnormal to me because I'd only been close to a few of my teammates but the 1996 Kentucky team would be the closet family I ever had while playing basketball.

The reason we won so often was because of our bond. We never let bitterness or jealousy interfere with our main goal of winning a championship. The season was considered the best season that the University of Kentucky men's basketball teams ever had and it showed. We swept the South Eastern Conference with a 16-0 record, sustained a 27 game winning streak, scored 86 points in one half, and had an average margin of 25 points per game. The numbers were amazing for any era of college basketball and it was humbling to be a part of that dynasty.

My small but close family began to show up to many of my games. Uncle George and Mark Masser actually became good friends. There were occasions that I'd take my son to the games. My teammates thought he was my little brother until I told them he was my son, they'd look at me in complete disbelief. Actually, no one believed that I had an eight-year old son but I wasn't ashamed because at least he was able to see how hard I worked to make it. Another good thing was that neither of us had to worry about having something to eat.

Those memories only added to the best year I had up until the moment we won the 1996 NCAA Championship! When we entered the locker room, I immediately went into the bathroom, stood in the mirror and said a quick, "Thank You," to God. I never forgot the promise I made to him, that if he'd ever give me the knowledge and strength to help myself, I would serve him forever. I did just that, and went back out and continued to celebrate with the team, my brothers.

It was my senior year and I had been the center of attention along with my best friend Ron Mercer. I was averaging 20 points and considered for Player of the Year honor along with Tim Duncan of Wake Forest. The season was going well and my relationship with my son and uncle were great.

There was one more thing on my list that I needed to prove to myself. I marked the date on my dorm room calendar and it was December 31st 1996. I put a red dot on it and then placed a big blue "X" on top of the dot. I was headed back to my hometown to play against the University of Louisville. The earlier games meant something to me because I craved winning but when I saw that date in the beginning of the season, I made it a point to work even harder the week of the game. No one ever knew that I secretly watched the Louisville team play so I could scout their weaknesses. I had a video guy make a tape of all the players in my position so I would learn their moves and see how they played defense on other opponents. The day of that particular game, I was on level ten, salivating for my chance to destroy the same team that neglected me a few years back.

Game day at Freedom Hall to play against the Louisville Cardinals was the day I anticipated for years. I entered the arena like a man possessed with one thing on my mind, winning that game! I knew I had to play harder than ever before, stay poised, and dismantle every player that got in my way. Once the game was set to begin I walked on the center of the court and greeted the opposing players with a smirk including my old friend Dequan Wheat who was now the star player for the Cardinals. I wasn't smiling like normal or even listening to the screaming Cardinal fans that surrounded the arena; I was already in the game.

The ball was tipped, we gained possession and I immediately took control by demanding the ball in the low post. I was guarded by a player that weighed almost thirty pounds more than me. However, I posted him up as if he was my son's size. I turned and dunked the ball with two hands. I had just made my statement displaying intense confidence. The next two plays were fast break dunks. I scored all but two of our ten points in the early part of the game. The play that released all my years of frustration and anger towards the Louisville program came right after a time out and I looked into the crowd and saw previous friends that were cheering against me. I sneered at them and went back onto the court. The Cardinals missed a shot and I sprinted up the sideline while my opponent jogged back. My teammate, Anthony Epps threw a low bounce pass up the floor and when I caught the ball, I saw two Louisville players back on defense. I took one dribble and my adrenaline exploded, launching me into the air with all my force. I slammed a one-handed dunk on the Louisville player.

I swung on the rim and looked at the Cardinal bench and the coach. Not one of them even glanced back at me. The coach turned away. I didn't hear a sound from anyone because I blocked everything and everyone out. My eyes presented the blueprint of how this game was going to begin and end.

We expanded our lead in the second half and defeated the Cardinals by twenty points. After the game the media came to interview me and all I said was, "I'm glad it's over." They didn't understand, but that was an affirmation that I'd finally moved on from being disrespectfully passed over. My focus was on finishing my season with another championship. That win felt so good and I watched it continuously for the next three days!

I had grown up feeling inadequate and was never good enough for anyone to want, but I wanted everyone to see that I was a worthwhile ... investment. Everything was steadily progressing and the team had started a ten game winning streak. We were all having fun just as we did the previous year.

After having a hard practice, I returned to my room to find mail from Columbus, Ohio. I had no idea what it could be because when I left, I didn't have any problems, disputes or anything. I opened the letter and as my eyes followed the words, it said I was a father. I had another son. I hadn't planned on hearing this type of news again, but it happened. Immediately, I called my ex-girlfriend from Columbus and we agreed to work things out. When we broke up that night, she was pregnant but didn't want to tell me because the breakup was on unfavorable terms. I was upset but it was imperative that I remained focused on my basketball career as well as my education. I only needed thirty hours to graduate and I didn't have any more eligibility to play basketball so I was on edge knowing I had to finish both of my goals that year.

The pressure didn't bother me because I was having a great season and things were going well for my team and I. However, I couldn't seem to escape fate. Every time my life gained promise and stability another twist of fate would disrupt my evolution of progress and happiness.

On January 18th, 1997, I felt as if I were back in that shelter home without the slightest trace of hope. We were playing the Auburn Tigers and I was leading our team into victory. Then everything came to a complete halt. I went for a loose ball, slipped on the floor, and hurt my right knee. I grabbed my knee, trying unsuccessfully, to convince myself that I wasn't hurt. So I got up and limped off the court and continued to try walking around for a while to make sure it wasn't as bad as it felt. I returned to the game but I could tell that my body wasn't responding to my mind anymore. The true test came when I drove baseline and went up for a dunk but *barely* made it over the rim. I lost hope and told the coaches, "Something's wrong with my knee." The doctors took me back to the locker room and hovered over me as they examined my knee over and over again. I couldn't tell if they were making sure I wasn't as bad as they thought or if they were trying to see which one was going to break the bad news to me.

The next morning was rough because my knee had swollen and I could barely walk. What made it worse was that I had to wait several hours before I received the results of my tests.

Coach Pitino slowly entered the room with a somber look on his face. He grabbed my shoulder like he was about to tell me I only had an hour to live. The doctor came over and said, "I'm sorry, Derek but you've torn your knee ligaments again." The pain I felt at that moment was worse than waking up without food, electricity, hot water, parents, or love from anyone. The word of my injury spread like a forest fire and all I kept hearing were people saying my career was over and I'd never make it to the NBA. They even said I would never score another point while at the University of Kentucky.

One day I was sitting in my dorm room and watched a movie called "Dead Poets Society," with Robin Williams. The movie depicted students thinking outside the box in order to accomplish what they've always wanted to do despite being told that they couldn't. At the end of the movie a kid took his own life because he felt he was never good enough to accomplish his dreams. After watching that movie, I said to myself, "I will never give up and I will never stop trying to be the best."

The same way I took the assistant's comments at the shelter home is the same way I took the news reporters words. I vowed to prove them ALL wrong!

* * *

Chapter 17

HOW BADLY DO YOU WANT TO SUCCEED?

This time, I had a different type of surgery by a phenomenal surgeon. He explained to me that this surgery was supposed to help me heal a lot faster and I wanted an expeditious return to good health. I started pushing myself to get better and worked hard to do my physical therapy ahead of schedule. My doctor knew how to motivate me and he knew precisely when to slow me down. He paced me well and taught me how to help my body heal and improve the restorative process. A great deal of the therapy was water training and I didn't swell like I had in the previous surgery. I was back and in excellent shape; ready to make medical history.

Finally, I was given the approval to shoot around with my teammates for a few days and see how things felt. Subsequently, I was cleared to practice with my team and a wave of relief took over. I savored this feat. The news reporters commenced with their barrage of questions. I'd proven to them that I was ready to play. I threw everything I had into working hard to reset that opportunity to get back on the court, focus on the game with my teammates again, and continue my definitive goal of playing in the NBA. The harder I worked on having accuracy, the more I became of interest to the media, as well. However, what I found purely inspirational was that the NBA scouts actually came to watch me workout. They needed to see if I was healthy enough to play both physically and mentally.

It was March of 1997 and we were in the Final Four playing a great game against the Minnesota Gophers. They were led by a Hall Of Fame coach, Clem Haskins, and had a future NBA Star, Bobby Jackson. The intensity was so high that my body adjusted right along with it. I was so ready to play!

The game went back and forth and the excitement remained high. The Gophers made a late charge but as they made a run, one of the Gopher players received a technical foul. Coach Pitino nearly ripped off his custom made suit jacket, took off running down our bench, and slid all the way to the end in his Gucci shoes to grab me to shoot the free throws. I was surprised yet, excited. For some reason, I wasn't nervous and I deem it was because I wanted that moment so badly that it had been resting heavily on my heart. The last time I heard my name called out in a college arena was two months prior to that very day. I had a job to do and could accomplish it at that precise moment. I had the ability to prove many people wrong and yet again, I did just that.

I spent a great deal of time developing mentally so that I could visually arrive at this point. It took years of determination and preparation to get here. My passion for having this type of game was unyielding and I allowed nothing to stop me. I walked up to the free throw line and drew in a deep breath as I gathered my thoughts preparing to savor the moment ahead of me. I stood behind that line and looked out into the sea of blue. Instantly, a powerful surge of confidence rushed back inside of me.

As a teenager, I'd challenge myself by shooting free throws alone and in the dark. I remained focused on the back of the rim because I'd been making all my free throws while barely able to see the goal. I said a prayer and thanked God for giving me the strength to make it to that point. I took my first free throw. It went up and ... in! The emotions of the Kentucky fans were completely unrestrained and grew louder as our opportunity moved closer. I didn't smile or show any emotion other than extreme focus.

Again, my concentration remained back at that moment of being alone in the dark focused on the back of the rim. As the official returned the ball to my hand, I realized, if I made this shot it could be my last, ending my college career. It felt as though the crowd felt the significance of that shot and grew silent. My teammates stared at me with the expectations of my leading them, just as I had done over the past two years. I bounced the ball twice, rolled my shoulders back, stuck my chin up in confidence just as my great-grandmother had taught me to do, and took my final shot as a Kentucky Wildcat. Swish! Until that point, I hadn't played in that game except to help earn those two critical points in the final four. I realized that I really wasn't trying to prove anything to anyone other than myself as I'd thought. Proving something to others was more of a reason to prove to myself that I could do anything if I worked hard for it. That game was all the motivation that I needed.

After advancing to the National Championship game for the second straight year, the media picked us to win the title, once again. We were playing the Arizona Wildcats, which was stacked with a talented group of players from, Mike Bibby, Michael Dickerson, Jason Terry, and Miles Simon. The game went back and forth for the duration and Miles Simon was having an incredible game. Ironically he played my position, which meant we would be guarding each other. I sat on the bench biting my towel in frustration locked on my visions of how I would shut him down on defense and utilize my strategy to completely destroy him on offense. Those visions remained that way because I *never* entered the game. We went into overtime and as I saw my teammates fighting to win the game, I couldn't help but try and get close to Coach P. and give my input on how to stop Miles from scoring. I told Coach Brooks to tell the guys to stop going for his ball fakes and attack him on offense. I was really trying to convince Coach to put me in the game for 5 minutes, but to no avail. As the time ticked off the clock, I sat at the end of the bench with a great deal of anger from the loss and from not being able to make a contribution to my team. Upon returning to the locker room it seemed as if every camera came running towards me. The primary question was, "Could you have played?" I told them it was really Coach Pitino's decision whether or not I played. I really wanted to tell them, "Hell yes, I could have played!" The only reason I didn't let the media know how badly I wanted to play was because the pressure would have been on Coach P. and he had really done so much for me that I wouldn't allow my own personal wants to hinder his ultimate wise decision of not risking my future.

I returned to my hotel room and sat on the edge of my bed trying to compose myself but couldn't manage it for anything after watching the highlights of the game. I snatched the television remote and slammed it against the wall. I exhaled deeply to try and calm down but it didn't help. I got up and went into the bathroom, leaned against the wall and stared into the mirror while the game played over and over again in my head. My eyes were red with fury and began to water. Although I tried, I couldn't accept the loss. Out of intense frustration, I released a tide of anger and screamed! This was the saddest day of my basketball career. Yet, I refused to allow that single moment in history to stop all of the many other great moments I had coming. I always dreamed of winning something that reflected hard work and dedication, but this one time I wasn't able to make a contribution to help end the defeat!

LIFE: Every time *I* felt like things were going well, life brought me back down to keep me where I needed to be. When I tried to do what I thought was right, it seemed as if things went wrong. It happens to us all but the difference is, either you make the choice to continue the fight to accomplish your goals or give up and lose with certainty. If you decide to give up, you will spend your life sitting on the bench watching others that have accomplished their dreams, found their purpose and are fulfilled.

People love winners because we see the intense passion and unwavering drive that we either have or are working towards embedding deep inside ourselves. The way we handle our adversities will be the way we live our lives. Once you decide to have faith in something, only you can change the outcome. I committed a long time ago to reject failure as a part of who I am. I decided to write the script for my own life instead of allowing someone else to write it for me.

* * *

Chapter 18

THE LAST LEVEL OF MY DREAMS

After going through the most rigorous workouts from several NBA teams, I finally received an invite to the NBA draft. I was prepared, motivated and excited because there were many people doubting me and questioning my physical health. Many of the skeptics were the same people that cheered for me just a few months prior.

Waiting to hear something was an unbearable feat because it was what I'd worked for and sought after so badly. I felt as if time were standing still. I sat in my dorm room the week prior to the draft refusing to watch any sports or news on television. I didn't have any interest in glancing at the newspaper until after the draft was over. I had not received a call and the pressure began to intensify. The feeling is inexpressible. I focused everything I had in me on having a career in basketball and gave credence to nothing else for backup. Now, my confidence was beginning to wane. I sat down and made a list of what I'd do if I didn't make it. It was difficult but it was something I hadn't thought of because I really never anticipated doing anything else, as this was my passion. *This was it!*

At that point, if basketball didn't work out I didn't have a contingency plan because I didn't know what else to do. My reality was still the same and would always remain obtainable because I believed in myself. Nothing really changed in that arena since I was a teenager. My goals were to graduate, get a good job, and take care of my children. Of course, a professional basketball player was the job I was passionate about and chose to focus on but my goals never changed because I've always had the mindset of working hard for everything I've ever wanted. Either way, I was certain things would work out.

Several days passed and I began to receive an abundance of calls from marketing companies. Since I wasn't confident that a career in basketball was an option, I had considered that my secondary objective would take me back to Louisville where I'd get a job. However, those plans were interrupted after I received a call from Nike.

Unexpectedly, I was invited to visit their headquarters in Portland, Oregon. My eyes lit up as soon as I entered the building and saw all of the shoes that I couldn't afford and the clothes I used to see my friends wearing while I wore the same recycled clothing every few days. It was a surreal moment and I felt like I'd awaken to birds chirping while I lay on the park bench. This was an overwhelming experience brought on by the discipline of having an amazing dream and working tirelessly to achieve it. My uncle George and I were ushered into a room and asked to have a seat outside of the conference room. Shortly thereafter, a gentleman approached us and then escorted us inside the conference room. We entered the room but I didn't scan the room to see who was there because I was taught to give eye contact when speaking to people. The first gentleman I met was Phil Knight, the owner of Nike, and he walked up to me and said, "Welcome to the team." After being stunned by his comment, I was approached by Michael Jordan. We were the same height and stood eye-to-eye at six-feet-six. His legacy was extraordinary and his career nothing less that brilliant. It was humbling. He spoke to me and actually knew my nickname "DA" as if we were friends. I had missed half my college season and lost in a Championship Game but I was selected by Michael Jordan to have my own signature shoe under the Brand Jordan company. The excitement I felt was unexplainable, but it didn't stop there.

It was draft day, June of 1997 and although it was a major accomplishment to become drafted, I was anxious to find out where I'd be drafted. The day arrived and I was sitting in the draft room waiting to hear my name called. The first name announced was Tim Duncan. Up until my injury, Tim and I were considered the two best players in college. At this point, I was patiently sitting in the waiting room listening to several names being called; although mine wasn't one of them I kept a smile on my face. As exasperating as it was I understood the game and the business behind it. From this point, I'd have to continue to compete for a position on the NBA platform and continuously strive to provide evidence that I belonged there.

The next pick called was my name. I was the 13th selected in the National Basketball Association draft, to the Cleveland Cavaliers. When I stood up, I felt the tension in my shoulders dissipate, my eyes widened along with my smile, and my heart stopped hurting from the pain of anticipation. No one other than God knew this outcome, but I had faith that I'd make it. This moment brought clarity. Every struggle I had, made me find a solution to end it. My child made me want something greater than I ever had for myself, which was a better life for him. Coach Pitino's characteristics as a coach had proven that his players came first. Although I didn't know it at the time, he knew there was interest in me but to make it to this point, I needed to be healthy. One injury could have kept me out of the draft. I didn't know then what I know now. As badly as I wanted to play in that last game as a Wildcat, Coach P. wanted me to have something more, a career in the NBA.

Uncle George didn't ever let go of me although he did let me go in order to learn invaluable life lessons that would shape and change the course of my life. He believed that there was more for me than what I could see at the time.

There were many times when I thought I was alone but it was preparation to acquire strength, discipline, truth, reality and faith. It happened. That life of uncertainty was no longer mine. I worked diligently to discover who I was and what God intended for me.

This would change my life.

I sat in my hotel all night with a million and one thoughts. I couldn't help but become emotional because I never thought my life could have changed this fast to this unimaginable degree. Success is achieved when you're dedicated to working hard at being successful. Positive results come when you implement the process of thinking and acting in a positive manner. Faith will appear when you believe in yourself. Trust that your faith will never lead you wrong when you are completely faithful and obedient to God.

I had the constant challenge of incessantly having to prove people wrong. Sometimes it took a lot out of me and it was hurtful having to do so. Knowing that people will bet against you to succeed is incomprehensible but a part of life. As time evolved, I grew wiser and accepted my reality; I wasn't doing it for them, but for me. I was proving to myself that I wouldn't fail. I needed to show myself that I was more than what people thought, which was nothing. I was proving that I am capable of achieving whatever I decide that to be. I take tremendous pride in knowing that I never lost myself in shame or pity.

I finally understood that my journey, inclusive of the sacrifices and struggles I encountered as a teenager, was a part of my test. The test, made me stronger, wiser, passionate, and took me from feeling hopeless to being filled with hope. It made me discover the reason I experienced sleeping on a park bench. I was meant to discover that I had a choice to quit or fight to fulfill my true destiny. It gave me faith! It was a necessary lesson and well worth the fight. I am ...

LIFE: Have you ever diverted your attention away from doing something that you passionately wanted to do because people were so discouraging and shared nothing but negativity about your goals? When you do that you may be releasing your gift from God. Don't let go of your dreams. The reason many of us don't reach our potential is because we don't believe in ourselves. Instead, we respond to jealously or envy. Many people love to dream but they are afraid to act upon those dreams and make them a reality. *I am not!*

* * *

Chapter 19

DIFFERENT LEVEL BUT SAME LIFE

The NBA provided an entirely different level to my life that was an experience in itself. I recall the day that I received my first NBA check. When I opened the white envelope I noticed the amount was for two hundred and fifty thousand dollars. This was the longest number I'd ever seen because I hadn't even memorized my social security number. These numbers were almost as long. As I stared at the check, my mouth dropped open. I wanted to know why nearly half of my money was gone? I wondered if I owed someone something or if I hired the wrong attorney. I picked up the phone, called my attorney and asked him, "Who the hell is FICA?" I found out that FICA was a newly found family member! I'd never been taught to comprehend tax implications but from this point I began the journey of understanding the financial world. The journey that God wanted me to fulfill was to believe in the abilities that I was born with. God wanted me to know that I was not what others saw but what He created. Playing in the NBA was never the point of my journey but a part of my growth. My growth progressed because I had stamina. My journey helped me to face reality regardless of how difficult and hopeless it seemed and to become a man of complete faith. *I am.*

While in the NBA I relocated back to my hometown of Louisville, Kentucky and started my own company so I could help those who once helped me, as well as, others along the way. My company was built to help the inner city low-income areas and create more jobs for those who wanted to better themselves. I used two million dollars of my own money to open two brand new strip plazas, refurbish three basketball courts that I used to play on, and then hired employees. I didn't know how to run a company but I was certain I could figure it out, as I had to do with most things. Because of all the injuries I had early in my career I knew basketball wasn't guaranteed forever so I planned accordingly.

It only took me a few weeks to get my Foundation started because it was something I was passionate about. I did it so the homeless and disadvantaged children would have a place to stay instead of sleeping on a park bench, or living in an abandoned apartment. I helped build up my neighborhood, had free picnics, gave away school supplies, and even put a shoe store in the heart of the inner city. Again I used my own money because I didn't want anyone to complain about how I was using others to help develop my city.

When I was homeless I was invisible to many and there are countless other invisible children, women, and men that need help. Those are the people I am seeking to make a difference for and want to reach because as long as they are out there, a part of me is, too. If you are willing, you are able. Everyone can do a little something to make a difference in someone's life. But don't ignore the plight of others as you never know if or in what capacity that may be you.

As time went on I had some great opportunities that caused me to make the decision to relocate to Atlanta. Before I left I received a call on my office phone from my brother. He told me that he was really sick and wanted to see me. I am a forgiving person and try not to hold grudges so I thought it was worth the effort to attempt to bring peace to our strained relationship before I left. I took my son with me because he had never met my brother. I thought twice about it, but took under consideration that if this could possibly be the last time I'd see him, I should go. I pulled up at his apartment and noticed my mother sitting on the steps. I sat in my car observing her for a few minutes while trying to figure out what was going on and then I realized that it was Mother's Day. The fact that I forgot Mother's Day meant I really didn't have the mindset or love to remember that holiday. I hadn't spent much time with my mother over the years, so this day wasn't any different. I saw my brother walk to the end of his porch to see if I was outside. As I looked at the both of them, the only thing that flooded back was pure negativity from our tumultuous and painful past.

They stared at my car, which had tinted windows, but were unable to see if I was inside. I watched my mother grip the handrail, stagger to her feet and head inside the apartment while my brother tried to grab hold of her arm to assist her. Unsympathetically, she jerked her arm away from him and I shook my head. Nothing had changed. I looked at my son and decided to drive off. It didn't appear as if my brother was really sick and I was certain my mother had no desire to see me. The cycle of pain was beginning to churn violently inside of me. It hurt to find my mother still in the same fragile place. I don't think she could or even wanted to face me. Instead of opening the door to a situation I couldn't fix or control, I did something I could and took my son to see a movie instead of dealing with the madness I had for so long. While we were there I went to the restroom and completely fell apart. The pain in my stomach was crippling but the stabbing in my heart was silently killing me. I was *still* tortured from the inability to make my mother love me. Even at this stage in my life and after everything I'd accomplished, I didn't have a mother! I couldn't accept the way she chose to live. She owed it to herself to fight for her life, like I was forced to do. It was emotionally jarring that we couldn't have a simple conversation that didn't end up being confrontational. It didn't matter what I'd accomplished or where I'd been, it didn't bring me what seemed like I waited a lifetime to have, a mother. To love someone that doesn't love you is painful, and even more when it's your parents because they are given our love, unconditionally.

I started to focus more on my Foundation and began to help children who were in my situation or worse. I hosted free picnics because I knew how it felt to be hungry and scrounging to find food. I gave away free clothing and shoes because I knew what it meant to be embarrassed wearing the wrong size shoes and wearing the same clothes for months. It was my way of dealing with my past deficiencies and emotions. I was trying to help those who wanted to help themselves. It was something my uncle George and Mark Masser taught me as I started to have success. They instilled in me the value of giving from your heart instead of your wallet. It was obvious that I could afford to give money but it meant more for me to actually be there to help unfortunate and helpless children. Seeing so many kids that reminded me of myself was hard enough. It was particularly difficult when I saw those who were giving up. That was something I couldn't ignore. My first trip to a shelter home was extremely emotional. I spoke to a small group of children that were acting out and having similar issues as I had. After I shared my personal story with them, one child gave me a hug. The young girl told me she was sorry about what I went through because I had it far worse than she did. She told me she has both of her parents in her life and that she would work towards changing because she knew she couldn't function without them. For some reason that was a defining moment in my life although I wasn't looking for it. I had made a difference to someone that needed guidance in the right direction.

* * *

Chapter 20

TIME WILL CHANGE YOU

The summer was ending and I was headed back to my NBA team to get ready for the season but I was still contemplating leaving Kentucky. I had a talk with a friend of mine from Louisville who was close to Muhammad Ali. He told me that I should think about going to a bigger city because it's good being one of a few fish in the sea but it gets stressful when you're the only fish in the pond. He explained to me that if I wanted to grow I would have to go somewhere that I could be in the few and then come back to bring others up with me. He shared one more piece of advice that I didn't notice until years later. He told me that when you want to better yourself be prepared to first get criticized, and then talked about me leaving. Plenty of lies will come because no one will really know why you left. They will miss you because they'll begin to understand that you were actually a good thing for everyone and wish you were back. He said, once I leave I'll be happier because no one judges you when they don't know you. It happens to a lot of people and it happened to me as soon as I left. The best thing that I did was to leave and make myself happy first so I could return to those who actually wanted to help themselves.

I packed my things and headed to Atlanta to start my new career in the movie business. I was changing for the better as I had closed most of my businesses in Kentucky and started my new company called Loyalty Media Group. From the time I was locked out of the apartment and allowed my creative thoughts to distract me from my disparaging reality, I enjoyed writing, and decided to expand my thoughts. With great passion, I put them on paper and into music.

My son graduated from high school, and was living with me full time. My mother and I hadn't spoken in quite some time and my father had become distant again. Things were changing but so was my maturity.

It was 2006 and I had just won the NBA championship with the Miami Heat. I returned to Louisville to celebrate with my friends and family. I went to visit my father and he confessed that he didn't have long to live. The cancer had significantly metastasized and he didn't want to endure any more treatments. I had a hard time accepting his position, to give in, but it wasn't my choice. He didn't look bad but the pain was so overwhelming that he could barely mutter but a few words. Only a couple of weeks after that visit, I received the call about my father passing. The pain was greater than I imagined because I never heard my father tell me *he loved me.*

Even after all my success and my accomplishments, I realized that the one thing I could never win was the love I longed for from my parents. It was hurtful that my career had come to an end and while having achieved a great deal, I never succeeded in having memories of my parents supporting or sharing in my accomplishments but it didn't stop me from loving my parents more than I love life itself.

Regardless of their struggles, I only have one set of

parents and I will always respect and love them through anything!

My brother and I have begun to rebuild our relationship and remain focused on being good friends again. My little sister and I have established a new relationship and I love every minute of watching her grow. After making a stronger effort to change her life, my mother and I have become closer than ever and on December 25th 2012; we had Christmas dinner together for the first time in twenty-eight years! My thoughts drifted back to the last dinner of my childhood that we shared many years ago. I held onto every piece of inspiration that I could find from my youth and used it for motivation believing that one day things would change ...

Given the way my life began, I had achieved several accomplishments as far as my education, championships, awards, financial success, and being a father. My life was peaceful. For the first time, I felt

that my mother and I had a real bond. God brought my life full circle. Because I had forgiven my parents and worked to allow God to direct my steps instead of my anger, he gave me a gift more valuable than one would know. He allowed me to hug my father one last time and to kiss my mother's chubby cheeks. I was waiting for those three words that remained unspoken, and although they never came, I received authentic expressions of love instead.

There were numerous blessings that came from the many challenges I had throughout my life. I

realized that my uncle George was the man that taught me to be a man and is the man that I call, *my father*. The Masser family has shown me what family really means. Having the privilege to watch them display family values provided a knowledge that I practice in my family. My relationship with my son Derek Jr. is so strong that we communicate daily. I thank God for guiding me to break the cycle so that neither he nor any of my children would ever repeat it. I am committed to growing stronger and staying close with all of my children. The days of my past are forgiven, and will remain history, although the loss of time and love still brings hurt. I pray that my story inspires and motivates you to have staying power through it all. This is my life and the experiences from my past, regardless of how traumatic, won't allow me to give in or give up because I have *Stamina*!

SPECIAL LOVE TO:

Muhammad Ali, Delores & Author Knight, Michael Jordan, Barry Murdock, Ray Lewis, Nicole Anderson, Terrance Moorman, Percy Miller, Kevin Judd & The Judd Family, Rajon Rondo, Dray Flynn, Rick Pitino, Dre Powell, Tyrese Gibson, Ric Elias and Family, Margo & Mo Dawson, DeJu'Nae Wicks-Edmonds, Ving Rhames, Chuck & The Mitchell Family, Mike Vine and The Vine Family, Anthony Boswell, Leland Taylor, Emmit, Karen and The Watsons, The Hughes Family, Glenda Williams, Margia Williams, Charles and The Nance Family, Christina Clark, Greg Jefferson, E. Wise, Gerald Thomas, Reese Gaines, James Curtis, Devona Wicks, Trevis Smith, Dino Carter, Alhaji Mohammed, Rickey Dudley, Reggie Rice, Dontaye Penny, Coach Randy Ayers, Coach Dave Cecutti, Keith Booker, The Breed Family, Tony Christiansen, Joe and The Irakane Family, The Holt Family, Keith Collins, Andre Gilkey, Derrick Plair, Andre Cochran, Tony Williams, Aaron Lee Starks and Family, Darnell Archie, Larry O'Bannon, Stephen Collier, Troy Gray, Kam, Paul Mamon, Antwon Parker, Brandon Alexander Hodge, Kenzo, DeWayne Metcalf, Antoine Brown, Tony Johnson, Howard White, Horace Rhodes, Derrek Hamilton, Chris, Brian Cox, JoAnn Mudd-Wise, Charlie Mudd, James A. Thompson Sr., Paul Mullins, Jonathan Berkley Sr. and Jr., The Finney Family, The Brooks Family, Anthony Ferguson, Eric Jackson, Mike, Jakki Dee, Ken Williams, Jermaine Hall, Reggie Gaston, Lee Taylor, LaMont Smith, Lincoln and The Satram Family, The Payne Family, Uncle Robert and

The Young Family, The Entire Big Blue Nation of Kentucky, and to ALL those that have come in contact with me to help me to this point, I say THANK YOU and I LOVE YOU!

MY RESTING FRIENDS AND FAMILY:

Clara Woolfolk, Maxime Montgomery, Mary Williams, Thomas Williams, Yolanda Williams, Maurice Williams, Bill White, Linda Daniels, Jason Gwynn, Leon Mudd, Antwan Stewart, Kentrail Robbins.